Slave Revolts in Puerto Rico

Winner of the
Puerto Rico PEN Club Award

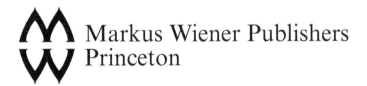

Markus Wiener Publishers
Princeton

SLAVE REVOLTS IN PUERTO RICO

Conspiracies and Uprisings, 1795–1873

GUILLERMO A. BARALT

Translated from Spanish by
Christine Ayorinde

For information, write to:
Markus Wiener Publishers
231 Nassau Street, Princeton, NJ 08542
www.markuswiener.com

Library of Congress Cataloging-in-Publication Data

Baralt, Guillermo A., 1948-
  [Esclavos rebeldes. English]
  Slave revolts in Puerto Rico : conspiracies and uprisings, 1795-1873 /
Guillermo A Baralt ; translated by Christine R. Ayorinde.
  Includes bibliographical references and index.
  ISBN 978-1-55876-463-7 (paperback : alk. paper)
  1. Slave insurrections—Puerto Rico—History. 2. Slavery—Puerto Rico—History.
  3. Puerto Rico—History—To 1898. I. Title. HT1086.B3713 2007
  306.3'62097295—dc22
  2007033366

Markus Wiener Publishers books are printed in the United States of America on acid-
free paper, and meet the guidelines for permanence and durability of the Committee on
Production Guidelines for Book Longevity of the Council on Library Resources.

Contents

Preface to the
First English-Language Edition

In 1985, when *Esclavos Rebeldes* was first published, it caused a stir on the island of Puerto Rico. As fellow historian Fernando Picó has written, *Esclavos Rebeldes* soon became a classic in Puerto Rican history. Up until the book's publication, the conventional wisdom was that slaves in Puerto Rico were docile, had no reason to rebel, and were generally treated well. Slave masters adhered to Spanish slave codes. Nevertheless, as *Esclavos Rebeldes* demonstrated, researching the municipal records of many towns on the island during the period between 1796 and 1848 revealed a radically different story.

In my research, I unearthed accounts of more than twenty slave conspiracies to take over the island, a great number of overseers murdered by slaves, and a high incidence of runaway slaves. This was only the beginning of what should have been many more years of research on the topic. Nevertheless, following the publication of *Esclavos Rebeldes*, I used the private historical records of the Vives family and those of the municipality of Ponce to write *Buena Vista: Life and Work on a Puerto Rican Hacienda 1833-1904* (1988). In my research for that book, I uncovered more than eighty-five runaway slave incidents between 1850 and1864—incidents that corroborated many of my conclusions in *Esclavos Rebeldes*. But I also concluded that since most of the slaves of Buena Vista had been born in the slave quarters of the hacienda and had had no exposure to the libertarian ideas of the African-born slaves, there was never a conspiracy on the estate.

Buena Vista was not a sugar hacienda but an *estancia* of minor crops, a corn mill, and a small coffee plantation. In this *estancia*, slaves worked amid more than forty minor crops and, unlike the slaves on the coast, had access to plenty of fresh water, since the Canas River crosses the Vives property. Later, I wrote an essay on the history of slavery on Hacienda La Esperanza, Manatí (1804-1873), published in 1989. Its owner was Jose Ramón Fernández, Marquéz de la Esperanza, one of the largest slave masters in the island and the most important and influential leader of the opposition to the abolition of slavery in Puerto Rico. As far as I know, there were no slave conspiracies or rebellions in this technologically advanced sugar hacienda, even after March of 1873, when the Marquéz de la Esperanza forbade slaves to leave the hacienda after abolition had been decreed by the Spanish courts. Of course, concluding on this basis that slaves on the island were docile or rebellious is much too simplistic. Slave rebellions were not an automatic phenomenon, and the factors contributing to them were far more complex.

In the years following the publication of these historical essays, my research began to center on the social and economic history of Puerto Rico during the twentieth century, taking me far away from the topic of slavery. Many questions remain unanswered about slave rebellions and conspiracies in Puerto Rico, and thousands of municipal records on this topic are yet to be discovered and analyzed. For these reasons, I welcome the translation of *Esclavos Rebeldes* into English. It may possibly provide the impetus for renewed research on the topic by a new generation of readers and scholars, who will undoubtedly uncover more acts of slave conspiracy and rebellion in Puerto Rico.

Guillermo A. Baralt
August 2007

Acknowledgments

This study has been made possible by the contributions of a large number of historians and friends. Especially deserving of mention is Professor John Coatsworth, the main reader of the original version of this book--a doctoral thesis submitted to the University of Chicago. It was Professor Coatsworth who encouraged me to study social and economic history. Professors Arturo Morales Carrión, Benjamín Nistal, and Carmen Rafucci guided my initial compilation of primary sources; Professor Luis de la Rosa of the Archivo General de Puerto Rico read the first draft of the chapters on Vega Baja and Toa Baja and provided me with the sound guidance that helped me uncover incidents that remained unknown until today. Professor Andrés Ramos Mattei suggested changes and offered important criticisms of the chapter on the history of sugar in Puerto Rico. Professors Gervasio García Rodríguez, Humberto García Muñoz, and Francisco Moscoso read parts of the original draft and provided invaluable criticism and observations. Mrs. Sybil Farrell de Lewis offered me many useful pieces of advice, and Professor Luce López-Baralt was of great assistance with the final editing of the manuscript.

I thank all of them very much for their generosity and help.

Abbreviations

AGPR   Archivo General de Puerto Rico.
              General Archive of Puerto Rico

AHN   Archivo Histórico Nacional, Spain.
              National Historical Archive, Spain

AMB   Archivo Municipal de Bayamón.
              Municipal Archive of Bayamón

AMG   Archivo Municipal de Guayama.
              Municipal Archive of Guayama

AMM   Archivo Municipal de Manatí.
              Municipal Archive of Manatí

AMP   Archivo Municipal de Ponce.
              Municipal Archive of Ponce

AMVB   Archivo Municipal de Vega Baja.
              Municipal Archive of Vega Baja

CIH   Centro de Investigaciones Históricas,
              Universidad de Puerto Rico.
              Center of Historical Investigations,
              University of Puerto Rico

Introduction

Until recently, only a very few of the slave conspiracies and revolts that occurred throughout the nineteenth century were known about. However, this book, which draws mainly on primary sources from several Puerto Rican municipalities, reveals that, counter to the prevailing view, slaves on the island rebelled frequently. The number of known conspiracies to seize possession of the towns and of the island, plus incidents in which whites and particularly *mayordomos* were murdered, is in excess of forty. But, given the covert and clandestine nature of these movements, the total is undoubtedly much higher. There were also hundreds of individual escapes that occurred on a daily basis and which represented another form of rebellion against the institution of slavery.

The main reason for the conspiracies was undoubtedly the excessive workload and the ill treatment experienced by the slaves. Nevertheless, the immediate causes of a particular incident and the reasons why it occurred in a specific place and at a specific time varied greatly. This explains why it has been so important to uncover incidents that were previously unknown. Equally important is the fact that it enables us to illuminate the social, economic, and political environment that produced these conspiracies. To this end, I have consulted all the available municipal documents. These include volumes of the Actas de Ayuntamiento [Town Council Proceedings]; Planillas de Riqueza Agrícola, Industrial, Pecuaria, y Comercial [Accounts of Agricultural, Industrial, Livestock, and Commercial Assets]; Protocolos Notariales [Notarial Records]; and many other files from the districts where there were conspiracies and uprisings. These documents enabled me to find out who the rebellious slaves were, whether they were *bozales* or Creoles, if they were all from the same ethnic group, who their masters were, the dates when they were bought and sold, which slaves acted as informers, and what other conspiracies had previously taken place in a particular district or on the island. From the same sources we can discover the economic circumstances of a hacienda, a *barrio,* or the country, that is, the conditions that gave rise to these conspiracies and revolts.

This research is merely the first step, as many of these incidents, which occurred over three hundred years of Puerto Rican history— from the sixteenth to the eighteenth centuries, a period during which there were undoubtedly other conspiracies and perhaps even uprisings that are yet to be unearthed—require further, more detailed research. Moreover, given that information in the available documentation is often limited, ambiguous, and frequently full of exaggerations, this book raises almost as many questions as it endeavors to resolve.

CHAPTER

I

The Seditious Seeds of Haiti and the 1795 Slave Conspiracy in Aguadilla

PUERTO RICO – MAJOR TOWNS AND CITIES

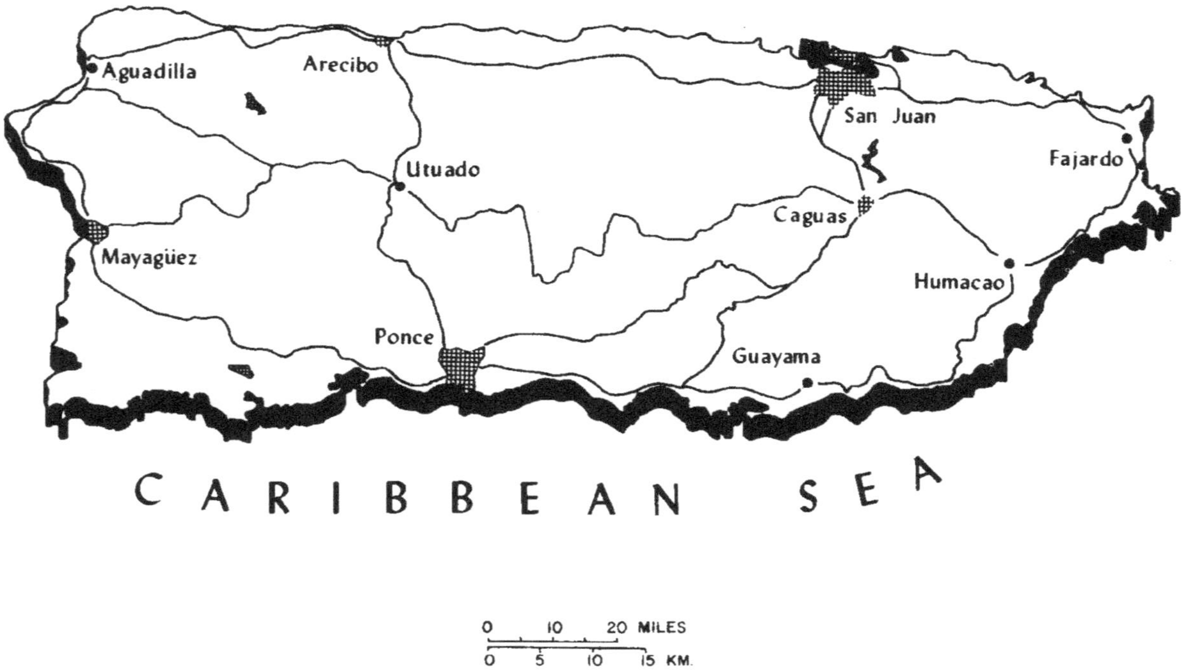

Fajardo

Humacao

San Juan

Caguas

Guayama

Utuado

Arecibo

Ponce

Aguadilla

Mayagüez

CARIBBEAN SEA

0   10   20 MILES
0   5   10   15 KM.

As the first colonists of the island of Puerto Rico watched their dreams of golden riches recede, Spanish economic activities were undergoing an important transformation. In around 1540, sugar supplanted mining as the colony's main industry. The colonists' hopes of rapid enrichment began to rise once again and, by 1550, Governor Vallejo was already announcing happily that "previously the island was in decline because the mines were running low; now it is prosperous due to the sugar industry."[1]

From the founding of the first sugar mill in Añasco in 1517 up until the abolition of slavery in Puerto Rico in 1873, work on the sugar plantations was always linked to African slavery. Time and again the establishment of new sugarmills was accompanied by requests to purchase African slaves or their American descendants.

In the sixteenth century, Puerto Rico, the smallest island in the Greater Antilles, had fertile lands on the coast and other environmental conditions that were ideal for cultivating sugar cane. In the first half of the century the sugar industry also benefited from imperial support. Spain promoted its development by granting loans and tax exemptions to the prospective hacendados as well as permits to trade in slaves from Africa.[2] Nevertheless, the sugar industry in Puerto Rico, like its indispensable slavery means of production, developed very slowly between the sixteenth and the eighteenth centuries.[3] Although it gained in importance once the mines were exhausted, sugar was always a secondary item in the island's colonial economy.

The cornerstone of the economy was subsistence crops that were cultivated by free laborers or families rather than enslaved labor. Production was confined to smallholdings. Some peasants supplemented the subsistence farming with crops for the contraband trade, such as indigo, tobacco, cotton, cocoa and especially ginger. In contrast to the sugar industry, these did not require large amounts of initial capital, huge expanses of cleared land, foreign machinery, deep-draft ships capable of sailing to Europe, or, of course, slaves.

From 1790 onwards, the sugar economy of the island underwent a radical transformation. The number of slaves increased more rapidly than in previous years. Between 1789 and 1802 it doubled, from 11,260 to 24,591, as shown in Table I.

TABLE I
Slave Population of Puerto Rico (1779–1802)

Year	Mulattoes	Blacks	Total Slaves
1779	3,626	4,527	8,153
1789	4,657	6,603	11,260
1799	9,138	12,081	21,219
1802	11,258	13,333	24,591

The rise in the number of slaves and the sugar boom was due to several factors that are briefly summarized here. First, the partial removal of the Spanish trade monopoly; second, the creation of the Guipuzcoana Company; third, the liberalization of the slave trade from Africa; fourth, the increased demand for Puerto Rican sugar in the United States of North America during its war of independence; and finally, between 1789 and 1804, the virtual destruction of the sugar industry of the richest sugar colony in the Americas: French Saint Domingue. This paralyzed sugar production, leading to a shortage on the world market and a sudden rise in prices.[4] This accelerated the rate of growth of the sugar plantations in Puerto Rico from the end of the eighteenth century.

The repercussions of the Haitian Revolution on the island were not only apparent in the increasing number of sugar cane plantations, but also of those who worked them. Overall, the Revolution had a devastating impact on the slave population of the Caribbean.

The social repercussions of the Haitian Revolution in Puerto Rico (1795-1810)

During the course of the Haitian Revolution (1789-1804) and in particular during the period of reconstruction under Toussaint L'Ouverture (1793-1801), slaves in the Caribbean colonies of the European countries, roused by the example of the victory of their counterparts in Haiti, rebelled time and again: in Guadeloupe and Saint Lucia in 1794 and in Cuba and Venezuela in 1795.[5] In Puerto Rico slaves in Partido de Aguadilla attempted to rise up on October 15, 1795.[6] The governor of the island, Ramón de Castro, believing the insurrection might be linked to what was happening in Saint Domingue, ordered that a number of important measures be taken to counter the propaganda of the supreme French libertarians.[7]

Although the insurrection in Aguadilla failed, it created a state of fear and alert in the Spanish authorities in Puerto Rico. They took preventive measures that were perhaps unnecessary, but, according to Governor de Castro they were justified on account of the critical situation in which the Government of Puerto Rico found itself.[8]

The most direct form of Haitian revolutionary influence in Puerto Rico over the following years was the use of emissaries and agents who were sent there to foment anarchy and disorder. We have documents referring to a Haitian agent named Chaulette who arrived in Puerto Rico in November 1805.[9] When this news was received, circulars were sent out to all the *tenientes a guerra* of the island's districts. The circular announced his arrival, describing him as a mulatto of 18 to 20, a polyglot speaking English, French and Spanish, of medium height and with curly hair. Governor Toribio Montes ordered his prompt arrest, before the agent "might spread his wicked seed in an island that enjoyed loyalty and calm."[10]

Months later, it was discovered that Chaulette's mission extended beyond the boundaries of the coasts of Puerto Rico. He was part of a general conspiracy of slaves in all the Caribbean colonies, coordinated from Haiti by the then-president, Dessalines.[11] Also, months later, there was mention of a conspiracy on the island of Trinidad.

One of the insurgents confessed under torture that there were people of color working against the subjugation of slavery and the prevailing order.

Although the government of Puerto Rico was aware that nothing significant had taken place, it decided to implement security measures, not only against the enslaved masses, but against free people of color, tramps and vagabonds, ex-convicts and other undesirable characters.[12] The Governor ordered that lists of the slaves be drawn up in each district, detailing where they gathered. He also asked that the conduct of foreigners and suspicious individuals be monitored and that a tally be kept of the number of weapons in Puerto Rico. Nine months later any colored man arriving from Santo Domingo was forbidden from landing and it was recommended that any who did disembark be arrested. The local judges were made responsible for arresting foreigners who entered illegally. If they failed to do so, charges were brought against them as well. Finally, the governor ordered that new residence permits [cédulas de vecindad] should not be granted to ex-convicts. These preventive measures were not only a reaction to Chaulette's failed conspiracy but also to the recent uprising in the district of Humacao, where slaves had attempted to take possession of the Casa del Rey [King's House] in that town.[13] Although we do not have any more information about this uprising, we believe that this incident must have been just as important as Dessalines' conspiracy. The Casa del Rey was the seat of administration for the government of each district. It was almost invariably situated in the urban area and was the place where the military garrison was stationed and hence where the arms of the urban militias were stored. Attacking the Casa del Rey represented not only a challenge to political authority, it was also the first stage of a process whereby, if the slaves were successful, they would take possession of the arms, leaving the urban militia defenseless. The history of the slave conspiracies in Puerto Rico confirms that prompt capture of the Casa del Rey was one of the main objectives in the plans for an uprising.

Dessalines' "accursed seeds" did not germinate in that year— 1806—and Chaulette was never captured by the Puerto Rican authorities. Nevertheless, in the years that followed, the *gobierno superior* continued to receive news of potential Haitian invasions. A year later, on November 13, 1807, the King of Spain wrote to Governor Salvador Meléndez alerting him to new plans for insurrection.[14] The King claimed he had received news that some of Dessalines' emissaries had set out from Haiti to organize a slave rebellion in all the American territories of the European provinces.[15] Governor Meléndez ordered that any Black man from Santo Domingo should be arrested.

On another occasion in 1810, Joaquín García, the governor of Santo Domingo, announced in a confidential letter to the governor of Puerto Rico that he had news of a Haitian plot to attack all the Spanish territories. García noted, moreover, that activity by the blacks had already been observed in Curacao and Jamaica.[16]

Twelve years later, in 1822, the government of Puerto Rico once again claimed to have information that President Boyer of Haiti was involved in the conspiracy being planned by Docoudray Holstein in the same year.[17] Three years later it was discovered that another Haitian emissary named Tristany was in Puerto Rico.[18]

These alleged incidents, like many others where the authorities stressed the involvement of Haitians, proved to be unfounded and unsubstantiated and only demonstrated the officials' enduring dread of the specter of the successful slave revolution there. Although we cannot discount the Haitian effect when discussing the Puerto Rican conspiracies, the immediate causes of these were the social and economic conditions of the places in which they occurred.

CHAPTER

▌▌

Major Disturbances in the Capital of Puerto Rico, 1812

The seeds of rebellion which were the subject of Governor Toribio Montes' nightmares, germinated when the first slave conspiracy broke out during the 1812 Christmas festivities. Slaves in the capital, San Juan Bautista, and the surrounding districts of El Roble, Guaynabo, Puerto Nuevo and Bayamón claimed that the Spanish Cortes Extraordinarias had decreed their freedom and that the Government of Puerto Rico was concealing this fact. However, this welcome news was not true. The Cortes Extraordinarias had not ordered the abolition of the institution of slavery. One of the reasons for this unfortunate confusion was a bill proposed by the Mexican member of the Cortes, Manuel Guridi Alcocer for the immediate abolition of the slave trade, which he presented to the Cortes Extraordinarias. This advocated freeing all children born to slave mothers, paying wages to slaves, giving the slave the right to buy his freedom as well as better treatment for those who remained enslaved.[19] Two months later, Agustín Argüelles, a Spanish member of the Cortes, announced the presentation of another bill, even more radical than that of Guridi y Alcocer. It proposed ending not only the slave trade but also the institution of slavery.[20]

Although both proposals agreed that public discussions should be held, they aroused a great deal of alarm in Spain. The proposals were never discussed nor approved by the Cortes.

The Puerto Rican member of the Cortes, Ramón Power y Giralt, who had been present at the meeting of the Cortes, sent a letter to his mother, Dona Josefa Giralt, who lived in the Barrio Puerto Nuevo of the capital. In it he asked that she be the first person to grant freedom to her slaves if this were agreed by the government.[21] On reading the letter, Dona Josefa began to cry and proceeded to tear it up. Power's mother was apparently reading the letter out loud while two of her slaves, Jacinto and Fermín watched the whole performance from a window. They understood the letter to say that slavery had been abolished in Spain.[22]

Jacinto and Fermín immediately ran away from the hacienda and announced the news to other slaves, Romualdo and Margarita, who belonged to Francisco Ruiz. They in turn informed another slave, Antonio, who was owned by Pablo Catalá. He already knew about the alleged events because Marcial, a slave of Maria Gertudis Lapuente who was also from Puerto Nuevo, had told him that this lady also had a son in Spain who had mentioned the same piece of news.

This information was also being spread by Benito, a carpenter on the "El Cazador," a brig of his majesty's mail. On arriving at the port of the capital, he circulated the false rumor that the "Cortes Generales y Extraordinarias de la Nación had granted the black slaves their freedom."[23]

According to the edict published on January 7, 1812, the purpose of the voyage of the "El Cazador" was to collect a special tax to help finance the struggle against the Napoleonic domination of Spain. However, Benito announced that the ship brought news of the abolition of slavery in Spain and that the island's government was suppressing this important favor. Both he and the slaves gave an unfortunate interpretation this proclamation. Drawn by the good news, groups of slaves from the town of El Roble to the south of the capital gathered in the square on the eve of the Epiphany festivities. At this meeting, Antonio Charboniel, a Haitian emigrant owned by Lorenzo Kercadó, announced that slaves were already free. Antonio de Castro, owned by Guzmán de Castro, stated quite harshly and vehemently that, "if they do not grant you their freedom now, as when they offered it to you during the siege of the English in 1797, more blood will be shed than during the Revolution of Guarico."[24] Nevertheless, not everyone present supported the instigators' declarations. Carolina, a slave of Madame Morín who was also from El Roble, immediately informed her owner that slaves in the capital were planning a general uprising, along with those from the countryside. Morín immediately relayed this news to Don Manuel Hernaiz, the Regidor Alguacil Mayor, and Don Rafael Chico, the Sargento Mayor de la Plaza, of the news. Several slaves were arrested forthwith.

Although the initial statements of the accused turned out to be untrue, it was agreed that terror should be instilled in the enslaved population in order to intimidate them, disabuse them of their error and compel them to set aside their wicked ideas. Eight of them were punished with the lash so as to teach them a lesson. It is possible that the extreme reaction of the authorities was due to the large concentration of blacks in the town of El Roble and surrounding areas. According to the census of 1812, over half of the inhabitants of El Roble were black. Out of a total of 1,282, 434 were white, 361 were free mulattoes and 257 were day laborers. A black uprising would therefore be disastrous for the inhabitants of this area and particularly for those in the capital. Moreover, El Roble was located to the south of the district of Cangrejos, a refuge for maroons and a place that was inhabited by black people.[25]

The plot spread rapidly throughout the entire northeastern region of the island. In Guaynabo, to the south of the capital, a black man, Juan Agapito del Rosario, was badly injured by militiamen for presenting armed resistance to imprisonment. He was suspected of fomenting unrest among the slaves on the banks of the Guaynabo River.[26] It was also suspected that Juan Luis, the mulatto slave of Gregorio Sandoval, was spreading other seditious rumors. Commissions were immediately set up to investigate these.

The conspiracy spread from the districts immediately adjoining to San Juan to the east—the district of Bayamón. There two free *morenos* were disseminating subversive rumors. The *liberto* Miguel García from Toa Baja urged Simón and Casimiro, slaves of Esteban Alcalá from Bayamón, not to be foolish by continuing to work despite being free. He encouraged then to join forces with him as all the slaves in his district, Toa Baja, had already been freed.[27]

Also in Bayamón, Facundo Astacio was urging some black slaves of Vicente Andino, the Captain of the Bayamón Milicias Disciplinadas himself, and of Dona Monserrate Dávila to revolt, telling them that "freedom had come to the slaves from the Cortes and the whites had usurped it and that they should start by organizing an uprising to obtain it."[28]

On January 14, the governor drew up a plan for defending the fields, haciendas and urban areas of the whole island. He apparently attributed great importance to the jails where some of the conspirators were already being held, as he assigned a large number of urban militiamen to guard them.[29] He also implemented precautionary measures which had the effect of turning almost every free citizen of Puerto Rico into a slave warder.[30] The governor also ordered that if a slave was discovered being disrespectful to his master or found away from his hacienda without permission, neither weapons nor machetes should be used. Instead he would be given fifty lashes by the Teniente de Guerra and then returned to his master's hacienda.[31] If the slave was the leader of a rebellion or had committed some outrage or violent act, he would be given a hundred lashes and sent to jail.[32] Every inhabitant was empowered to apprehend and bring before the district judge any slave or free person "about whom he was suspicious or who induces the blacks to believe they are free."[33] It was ordered that a permanent day and night watch to be set up in every quarter of each district. Meetings of more than three blacks were also prohibited. If a group consisted of five people, the gathering was regarded suspicious and its purpose investigated.[34] Masters were to be responsible for their slaves and, finally, no inhabitant could travel through the countryside of his district "without the permission of this government or of the judge of the territory."[35]

The immediate military response, which was effective if perhaps extreme, reflected the terror inspired by the news that were on the island many slaves who had been trained in Santo Domingo during the catastrophe of El Guarico.[36] Governor Meléndez Bruna pointed out that news of the "ascendancy assumed by the people of color in Venezuela, and it is in the Antilles a very great evil to have seen the black Christophe set himself up as the King of Haiti, with white servants" was also not agreeable.[37]

In addition to the military mobilization was the cooperation of the white citizenry who were particularly fearful of their own interests and welfare.[38] On January 30, 1812, the governor re-established the companies of urban militias and formed a battalion of whites named the "Voluntarios de la patria" [volunteers of the fatherland]. In the years that followed, the government received news of further rebellious outbreaks in places as far from the capital as Aguadilla, San Germán, and Cabo Rojo to the west of the island. As the false rumors spread from the capital, the confusion multiplied. In Aguadilla, a slave by the name of Juan Evangelista, who belonged to María Manuela Segarra, declared that his stepfather Miguel Bilbao had informed him that he received an order that all the enslaved blacks should be free.[39] The order was from the Black King, Henri Christophe in the French part of Santo Domingo. Bilbao stated that the rumor that the foreign blacks would be free was spreading through Aguadilla.[40] In the district of San Germán, Captain Juan Dávila reported that Juan Miguel Cancel, a slave of Luisa Cancel, had said that the Regency had already declared that the slaves should be freed and that "Atanacio Ortiz had assured them that there was no longer slavery."[41]

At the end of January, as noted earlier, statements were taken in different parts of the island from at least twenty-six blacks accused of conspiracy, plotting, assembly and alleged uprising. On February 4, in order to ensure greater security for the loyal inhabitants of the island, it was decided that, after they had served their respective sentences, the following slaves should not remain in Puerto Rico or the Spanish dominions: Juan Luis (owned by Gregorio Sandoval), Antonio (owned by Germán de Castro), Josef Pua (owned by Luis Yumet), and Juan Evangelista (owned by Manuela Segarra).[42]

The freeman Antonio Ortiz was sentenced to a year of labor in public works. An additional eleven slaves were punished in the pillory, "three with fifty lashes and eight with thirty." Jacinto and Fermín, slaves of Dona Josefa Giralt, and Marcial, owned by María Gertrudis de la Puente, were acquitted as, according to the statement there had been no seditious intent. They had simply passed on what they had heard. However, it was ordered that their masters keep an eye on their activities to avoid "the spark that was believed to be extinguished" being ignited once more in their haciendas and taking a dangerous turn on the island.[43]

The punishments meted out to the conspirators as a deterrent, although in some cases unjustified, were generally not harsh. For example, Lorenzo and Jaime, slaves of J Byrne, were returned to their master to be instructed in the Catholic religion. Although the authorities were apprehensive in the initial days when the statements were being taken, they were ultimately only interested in ensuring that the slaves realized that everything had been a misunderstanding. None of the conspirators were sentenced to death. This restrained response, which showed considerable understanding of the motives of the "poor wretches who groan in slavery", as Governor Meléndez Bruna out it, can be observed from January 20 onwards, at the precise moment when the cause of the conspiracy was already clear and it was understood that it had all been a mistake. Most of the slaves therefore ended up being acquitted.

At the same time as these events were taking place in Puerto Rico, slaves in Havana, Cuba who learned of the rejection of the abolitionist bills in March 1811 began a large-scale conspiracy.[44] The leader was another carpenter by the name of José Antonio Aponte. Like Benito, he was adamant that the Cuban hacienda owners and the island's authorities were attempting to conceal the important news of the abolition of slavery. As happened in Puerto Rico, the authorities claimed Haitian involvement, via a black man called Jean François. Free blacks took part in both conspiracies, which were uncovered, but, whereas in Puerto Rico the danger quickly abated and there was no unfortunate flare-ups, in Cuba there were violent rebellions.

The insurgent Cuban slaves destroyed canefields, coffee plantations and other cultivated land. Finally, whereas the punishments in Puerto Rico had been light, in Cuba five free blacks and three slaves were hanged.

Months later, in Spanish Santo Domingo there was another insurrection following unfounded rumors that Spain had abolished slavery and the local authorities were suppressing it.

All of these conspiracies indicate that, although the slaves received information about events in Haiti, Spain and other places where slavery was under discussion, the interpretation of the facts was frequently erroneous and gave rise to extraordinary misunderstandings. This happened either because it was based on clandestine information or secondhand rumors or out of an unmitigated desire for freedom.

CHAPTER

III

Bayamón, July 1821

The initial investigations carried out after the 1812 slave conspiracy in the vicinity of the capital revealed that a free *moreno* in the neighboring district of Bayamón had announced to some slaves of Don Vicente Andino and Doña Monserrate Dávila that "freedom had come to the slaves from the Cortes and the whites had deprived them of it and that they should begin by launching an uprising to obtain it."[45] On that occasion the slaves of Andino and Dona Monserrate did not rise up. However, nine years later, Marcos Xiorro, also owned by Andino, the captain of the *milicia disciplinada*, headed an alarming conspiracy against the white population of Bayamón in 1821. This was more threatening than the 1812 conspiracy because the economic and social conditions of that district had changed considerably.[46]

At the end of the eighteenth century, Bayamón had become one of the main sugar-producing regions of Puerto Rico. Large-scale development took place between 1810 and 1820 when there was a shortage on the world market following the destruction of many plantations in Haiti.[47] As result the price of an *arroba* of sugar increased from four to 28 *pesos*.[48] The government of Puerto Rico equipped ten ports throughout the island to facilitate the production and sale of sugar. The Spanish government promoted development of the industry by means of the *cédula* [charter] of 1815. This abolished some taxes, removed some import tariffs on slaves and machinery and encouraged white foreigners with capital to come to the island.[49] They were given land, exempted from paying some taxes for a number of years and permitted use their own ships for trading.

Encouraged by these conditions, the Bayamón landowners— Creoles, Spaniards and newly-arrived foreigners—considerably expanded the number of acres given over to cultivating cane. Between 1815 and 1820 eleven iron *trapiches* were imported to augment the seven wooden mills which were already in place by 1815.[50] There were also 16 stills. The number of slaves rose significantly, from 111 in 1765 to 1,086 in 1820. However, it was between 1815 and 1820 that the greatest increase took place, from 517 to 1,086.[51] "Bayamón was flooded with *bozal* slaves."

However, these were not years of unlimited development for all plantation owners. In Bayamón many hacendados' dreams of wealth never materialized. For example, Fernando Fernández, one of the leading hacendados in Bayamón and the owner of several slaves who took part in the conspiracy, complained in a letter to the *alcalde mayor* Don Miguel Andino, dated April 1821—two months before the conspiracy—that he did not have funds to pay the current *subsidio*.[52] In this letter Fernández stated that he could not meet his obligations because at that time the production of his hacienda no longer had any value.[53] He also pointed out that he would need to take a loan to cover the large outlay required by the plantation, particularly for sugar factories which were essential.[54] Fernández ended by stating that his debtors, in turn, had let him down, leaving him without any hope of receiving payment from them.

The conspiracy of Marcos Xiorro

In July 1821 while the sugar was being harvested in the district of Bayamón and the most arduous and demanding period of their work regime was drawing to a close, slaves from the district organized a conspiracy, along with others from the neighboring districts of Guaynabo and Río Piedras to the east and Toa Baja to the west. This was scheduled to begin at twelve midnight on Wednesday, July 29— the feast of Santiago.[55] The plans were as follows: several slaves from the McBean, Kortright, Andino, and Fernández haciendas in Bayamón, with the assistance of some *capataces* [overseers], would escape and head for a canefield at the hacienda of Miguel Figueres, also in Bayamón.[56] There they would find cutlasses and swords hidden in a bundle of cut cane which would be placed across the path in the canefield. Then, led by Mario, a slave and master sugarman from Angus McBean's hacienda, the Bayamón slaves would join forces with those from the haciendas of José Canales and Juan Reyes in Toa Baja to go and capture the town of Bayamón. Meanwhile, Mario would send the slave Juan Agustín to notify other conspirators in Toa Baja. Juanillo would do so at Antonia Ayala's hacienda in Río Piedras, and Pedro, who was owned by Antonio Ayala, would do the same at the San Patricio hacienda. The group from Bayamón would then divide into four, covering the four corners or entrances to the town. They would attack the houses of the alcalde, a Frenchman, and the priest. The attack would begin when they heard a signal given by firing off three rockets in the town. The reason for attacking these locations was to capture the arms—firearms and other weapons— which they knew were to be found there. Once armed, the insurgents would then set fire to the town and cut the throats of the whites.

After the town had been captured, the slaves, duly armed, would then set out for the capital. On the way they would split into two troops, one to be stationed on the bridge of Martín Peña, where the slaves from Río Piedras and Guaynabo would be waiting, and the other one at Palo Seco. The idea was to prevent the white inhabitants from leaving the city. Once victory was certain, they would head for the Mira Flores hill in the District of Cangrejos, very close to the capital. There Mario would be proclaimed king in the absence of Marcos Xiorro, the main ringleader of Bayamón.

Even though the conspiracy was well planned, the military mobilization that awaited the prospective rebels was even better organized as the authorities were alerted by an informer. Five days before the date chosen for starting the uprising, the slave Luis, a *capataz* at the Figueres hacienda, revealed plans of the conspiracy to Ambrosio, a Creole aged 22 and a trusted slave of Figueres.[57] There was an initial meeting between them during which Luis only divulged some of the details of the plan as he knew that Ambrosio was trusted by his master.[58] But at the second meeting, when Luis saw that Figueres had recently punished Ambrosio for injuring one of his oxen he realized that this made him a potential conspirator and decided to tell him everything. Ambrosio immediately notified his master, who informed Don Cayetano Náter, the alcalde of Bayamón.[59]

As soon as he had been informed of the conspiracy, Alcalde Náter ordered the military commander of Bayamón to place twenty armed soldiers at his disposal.[60] He also told the commander of the urban militia to put fifty men to guard the town. He ordered a search of the slaves' *bohíos* and an inspection of the canefields. He also told them to look out for the sign mentioned by Ambrosio in his denunciation. A day later, the total number of soldiers mobilized amounted to almost 500, including 350 urban militiamen, 98 infantry and 33 cavalrymen.[61] Firearms were distributed and the soldiers were stationed at eleven different locations, including the vicinity of the roads that led to the haciendas of Kortright, Ríos and McBean, the wharf, the roof of the parish church, bridges, jails and so forth. During the night of July 25, 1821, nothing of signficance occurred except for a slave throwing a stone from a banana plantation opposite Figueras' house. On the following morning the alcalde himself sent a group of militamen to search the canefields once more.[62]

* * *

After July 24 as soon as Ambrosio had reported the conspiracy, an investigation into the events began. Thanks to the detailed description provided by Ambrosio, and the rapid military mobilization, the ringleaders and the followers were captured immediately. Ambrosio's statement incriminated several slaves. Under interrogation they implicated others in turn, and so it went on. For example, in the investigation conducted on July 29, 1821, the governor of Puerto Rico himself, Arostegui, reported that Francisco, a slave of Juan Rijos, had informed him in his statement that Benito, of the same master, had said that Silvestre and Juan Loco were involved in the uprising.[63] Alejandro, owned by Laureano Rama, referred in his statement to four slaves who had been denounced by their master.[64] In addition, as a result of this rising tide of investigations, other incidents were discovered, although they were not connected to this conspiracy. For example, a month previously, one of the *bozal* slaves from Aranzamendi and another from Ramos had set fire to the bagasse building at Kortright's hacienda.[65]

On July 30 the following slaves had already been sent to the prisons of Bayamón: Fabián, Narciso, Vicente, and Ignacio, who belonged to José X Aranzamendi; Pedro Sebastian, owned by Antonio Ayala; Juan Agustín, belonging to McBean; Pedro and María Concepción, owned by Luis Canales. Days later the following were sent to jail in the capital: Arturo Ringo, Gaspar, and Cornelio, owned by Kortright; Juan Chiquito, owned by McBean; José María, owned by José N Cestero; Domingo, from the hacienda San Patricio; and Antonio and Pedro, overseers of the hacienda Las Monjas. A total of 61 slaves were arrested, as detailed in the following list:[66]

TABLE II
Rebellious Slaves, Bayamón (1821)

Master	Slave
1. D. Fernando Fernández	Crispín, Saviosa
2. D. Vicente Andino	Josef Joaquín, Marcos Alonso
3. D. Miguel Figueres	Eugenio, Felipe, Pedro, Luis—Capataz, Juan, Antonio, Laureano
4. D. Nicolás de Abila	Josef Luis
5. D. Josef Canales (Toa Baja)	Andrés, Antonio
6. Da. Juana Dávila	Antonio
7. D. Cayetano Náter	Marcelina
8. D. Juan Rijos	Josef, Francisco, Santiago, Elías, Lorenzo, Benito
9. D. Antonio Ramírez	Domingo (Hacienda de San Patricio)
10. D. Alexandro de Castro	Antonio Díaz, Pedro (Hacienda de Monjas)
11. D. Cornelio Kortright	King, Cornelio, Gayan, Antonio

TABLE II (Continued)
Rebellious Slaves, Bayamón (1821)

12. D. Juan Favier	Beltrán
13. D. Antonio Ramos	Domingo
14. D. Francisco Alexandro	Josef
15. D. Lorenzo St. Just	Santiago
16. D. Josef Xavier de Aranzamendi	Gavino, Vicente, Ignacio, Narciso
17. Da. Antonia Ayala	Pedro, Sebastián, Ramón
18. D. Angus McBean	Ylario Frances, Juan Agustín, Pedro Castañón, Josef Chiquito
19. D. Luis Canales	Pedro, María Concepción
20. D. Juan Landro	Apolinasio, Nicolás, Julián, Manuel. Merced, Alejandro
21. D. Manuel Dávila	Martín
22. D. Estevan	Beltrán
23. D. Nicolás Cesteros	Cirilo, Josef María
24. D. Laureano Ramos	Alexandro
25. Da. María Durascón (widow of Durán)	Gregorio, Alexis
26. D. Pedro Basallo	Luis, Juan

Source: AGPR. Fondo Documental de los Gobernadores. Gastos del juicio de los 61 esclavos que tramaron una Conspiración en Bayamón en 1822, Negociado y Seguridad Pública. E. 23, Caja 370.

One of McBean's slaves, Mario, a master sugarman and the future king and leader whom Ambrosio had identified as one of the main accomplices, was found ten days later, on August 2nd, hiding behind his *bohío* in a banana plantation.[67]

The absent king of Mira Flores, Marcos Xiorro, a slave of Vicente

Andino, the captain of the urban militia and, according to the authorities, the driving force behind the conspiracy, was captured on August 14 in Mayagüez after being wounded in the head by a cudgel.[68] In fact, the authorities knew that Marcos had been in Mayagüez for several weeks because on July 25 the alcalde of Bayamón wrote to his counterparts in Cabo Rojo and Mayagüez asking that Xiorro be captured dead or alive and taken to the capital.[69]

Marcos Xiorro's absence from Bayamón on the eve of the planned uprising, the night of 29 July, raises a number of important questions. What was the reason for his absence? Perhaps Xiorro was in Mayagüez attempting to incite slaves in that district to take part? Or, as appears more likely, he was there establishing links to military assistance from Haiti with the Bayamón rebels? This last hypothesis could be correct because, when they concluded their investigation into this conspiracy, the authorities suggested that President Boyer of Haiti had been involved in it. We do not know what sources they had for reaching this conclusion but, according to the Government of the island, Haiti was always a factor in the Puerto Rican slave conspiracies. Exaggeration or historical fact?

*   *   *

Several days after the July 25 conspiracy was uncovered, Governor Arostegui, aware that it was likely that slaves from the neighboring towns had been involved in the unsuccessful revolt, wrote to the alcaldes of Río Piedras, Guaynabo, Toa Alta, and Toa Baja informing them of the seditious plot.[70] He urged them to take preventive measures and asked them to warn the masters and to keep a watchful eye on the slaves, forbidding them to associate or leave their dwellings. He also made the hacendados responsible for the slaves' conduct. In Toa Baja on July 26, the alcalde José Córdova, hearing of the events in Bayamón, assembled what forces he could and made the hacendados divest "their respective domestic slaves of the tools needed for their labors and any instrument that might be offensive."[71] Although it remained quiet, for reasons that are unknown, seven slaves owned by the hacendado Juan Ríos and a slave of Lorenzo Borregrero were sent to jail in the capital.[72] Four slaves who were discovered away from their dwellings were also arrested but were not found guilty.[73] Their problem was that they did not have permits to leave their hacienda. The same thing happened in the district of Manatí where the authorities, suspecting that there was a branch of the Bayamón conspiracy in that town, arrested eight slaves following a military mobilization and sentenced them to jail.[74]

The initial reponse of the authorities seemed to be effective as, three days later Náter, the alcalde of Bayamón, requested that the urban militia to be reduced from 350 to 80 soldiers.[75] At the same time, and because he had arrested so many suspects, Náter was obliged to send those who were already in jail to the capital. In an attempt to expedite the proceedings and punish the accused, Náter agreed with the Auditor de Guerra that three *fiscales* should be nominated and that the suspects be distributed between them.[76] On August 15, the Court-Martial concluded the proceedings and sentenced 17 slaves to different punishments. Mario and Narciso were executed. Gregorio and Antonio were sentenced to six years' hard labor in San Juan. The masters of several slaves were given custody of them and made responsible for meting out the punishment pronounced by the Consejo. These were the following: Antonio, who belonged to Juana Dávila; Antonio and Juan, owned by Miguel Figueres; Alexis who belonged to María Durán; Arturo, Cornelio, and Gaspar, who were owned by Kortright; Santiago, belonging to St Just; Eusebio and Agustín, who belonged to Fernando Fernández; and José Lico, owned by Nicolás Dávila.[77]

The punishment given to Marcos Xiorro, the leader of the conspiracy is not mentioned in the statement. This may because he was captured on August 14 in Mayagüez and was tried separately. Nevertheless, wc do know for certain that he was not executed and that he may have been returned to his master to be punished.

After the inquiry had concluded, the ringleaders been executed and their followers punished, an argument broke out between the authorities and the hacendados who owned the 62 slaves who had been subjected to questioning. This was because the hacendados were refusing to pay the costs of the trial and maintenance for the slaves while they were in jail, as prescribed by the Código y Deberes de y Derechos de Dueños de Siervos, 1789.[78]

Escapes in Bayamón

The total failure of the conspiracy, the prompt and effective investigation by the military authorities, the punishment of the ringleaders and the denunciations made by the slaves themselves before the military tribunal explain why no more collective uprisings occurred in Bayamón and neighboring districts. Nevertheless, many of the slaves who took part in this conspiracy and even others who did not, decided to run away from their haciendas in the years that followed. For example, three years later on February 23, 1824, eight young slaves owned by Francisco Cepero, who were in Pueblo Viejo at the hacienda of Juan Sánchez, stole a pirogue and headed for Santo Domingo via the Bahía de la Capital.[79] The majority were young *bozales*. Four of the eight were of the mandinga *nación*, one was Carabalí, another Puerto Rican, and the rest of unknown origin. The escape came to an abrupt end when they were captured and returned to Bayamón by the captain of an English warship anchored in the Bahía de San Juan.[80]

In 1824, slaves from Juan Landrón's hacienda, who had also been questioned after the 1821 conspiracy, ran away.[81] Apparently on this occasion the slaves headed towards Corozal. Landrón immediately appealed to the alcalde because this was inconvenient for him particularly at a time when the sugar harvest was approaching.[82]

There was another escape by slaves in the neighboring district of Toa Baja, who plotted along with others from Bayamón. Toa Baja was a district with a strong revolutionary tradition. During the 1812 conspiracies in the capital and in Bayamón, various pre-emptive measures were taken anywhere that slaves from Toa Baja were to be found. Two years after the 1821 conspiracy, on July 4, 1823, during the festivities[83] in honor of Saint James, forty slaves ran away, taking advantage of the fact that the townspeople were distracted. Twenty of them belonged to Juan Primo, one was owned by Francisco García, two by Angel Marrero, six by Santiago Rapp, two by Luisa Marrero, one by Juana López and one by Silvestre.[84] There were also seven from the hacienda of José Canales in Bayamón, where slaves had taken part in the Bayamón conspiracy of July 1821. According to the military report, Pedro, the leader of the escape, was from the district of Arecibo, which although situated on the northern coast, lies far from Bayamón and Toa Baja. Future research could examine the connection between Pedro and the Toa Baja slaves, and between those owned by José Canales in Bayamón. Perhaps they were from the same African *nación*?

Finally, in 1826 other slaves at the hacienda of Don Manuel Dávila, also in Bayamón, planned an escape which was also unsuccessful. In July of the same year, slaves from several haciendas in Toa Baja and Bayamón joined forces once more to plan an escape with Haiti as its destination. Word of the conspiracy was disseminated among the slaves by means of a "bomba" sung by José Joaquín, a slave of Miguel Dávila in Bayamón. When he finished singing he asked for money, a boat for escaping to Haiti and goods and merchandise. He also invited others to flee with them.[85] It was said that another slave, known as Tío Bautista from the "El Plantaje" hacienda and owned by the Irishman Enrique Buist, was helping the conspirators spread the seditious message. It was in fact a child slave of Enrique Buist who informed his master of the escape plans when the latter arrived at his hacienda "El Plantaje" on July 18. Buist, in turn, reported the escape to the authorities, and proceeded to do everything in his power to thwart the plan. This proved effective because the escape was not carried out.

CHAPTER
IV

Docoudray Holstein and the Night of San Miguel

During the first half of the nineteenth century, the Spanish Empire in America had shrunk to only two colonies: Cuba and Puerto Rico. In Puerto Rico, the struggle for independence was characterized by pirate invasions, Haitian emissaries, and foreign adventurers who continually beleagured its coasts. Very little is known about these liberators—who they were and what their true intentions might have been. Similarly, there is very little information about the Puerto Rican liberation movement and its possible connection to these expeditions. Nevertheless, we do know about the fears of the Spanish officers and the measures taken by them to prevent these liberation expeditions from landing on the island, especially between 1820 and 1824. Two of these adventurers were Roberto Cofresí and Manuel Suárez.[86]

At the end of that same year another expedition was organized to create an independent Puerto Rico. According to the existing documentation, the Partido Revolucionario de Puerto Rico entrusted Docoudray Holstein with putting together a liberatory expedition. Holstein, a native of German Alsace, had fought in the Venezuelan independence wars. Simón Bolívar had commissioned him to defend the Fortaleza de Bocachica in Cartagena and promoted him to a high rank in the militia. However, the royalists had laid siege to the plaza, and Holstein consequently fell from favor. Filled with hatred, Holstein moved to the Dutch colony of Curaçao where, over the following three years, from 1819 to 1822, he passed the time giving piano and French lessons.[87] It was there that he was invited by the Partido Revolucionario in 1822 to prepare the expedition. Holstein moved to the northern United States to do so. In Philadelphia he wrote a manifesto inviting merchants and entrepreneurs in the United States to subsidize the expedition to set up the Republic of Boricua.[88] In it Holstein described Puerto Rico as a rich and fertile land which had not suffered from wars of independence. He also pointed out that it would be an excellent location for United States merchants to make a profit from their surplus merchandise.[89] His main aim was to establish free trade. But he also planned to form a government that was very different from those in the independent Latin American republics.

The manifesto of the Alsatian military man obtained the desired support as, from August 1822 onwards, several Philadelphia merchants, cadets at the West Point Military Academy, journalists, other foreign mercenaries and newspapers such as *The Columbian* and the *Washington City Gazette* were backing the expedition.[90] The number of supporters was between 200 and 400 adventurers who were ready to set out from various ports in the northern United States for the Añasco coast in the west of Puerto Rico. This conspiracy did not remain a secret. A month before the date arranged for deaparture, the Spanish authorities had already notified the Gobierno Superior of Puerto Rico of the planned conspiracy through their consuls in Philadelphia and New York. The Puerto Rican government suspected that, in addition to the support received in the United States, President Boyer of Haiti was backing the conspiracy, along with other Spanish American revolutionaries.[91] Ultimately, Holstein was planning to rely on support from the island's slaves.

Once news of this conspiracy reached the island, highly effective measures were taken to prevent the schooners from landing. In Añasco, where they planned to disembark, the military man Federico Garcen pointed out that the Compañías de Milicia de Infantería did not have a single operational gun and only had 100 cartridges sent by the Captain General 1821, and around 16 and 20 others which he himself had bought.[92] In fact, according to Garcen, the situation was much the same throughout the island. There were very few armaments and the western coasts did not have even the most basic elements for their effective defense. Communications were extremely poor and too much time and effort was required to bring together individuals separated by large distances.[93]

Sugar and slavery in Guayama (1800-1820)

The sugar boom of the beginning of the nineteenth century made the district of Guayama one of the most prosperous regions of Puerto Rico. Its coastal valleys were cleared and cane plantings covered its most fertile land. The best and most modern sugarmills were constructed to crush the cane, the port was fitted out and foreigners arrived, bringing the capital and technical knowhow for sugar production. During this period there was unprecedented development of sugar on the island.[94] At the same time, Guayama was flooded with "innumerable" *bozales*, who were brought to the island from Africa and who, along with American-born slaves, became the main source of labor for the plantations.[95] From 1802 to 1828 the number of Creole and African slaves tripled, from 669 to 2,373 (see Table III).

TABLE III
Slaves in Guayama (1779–1828)

Year	Number of Slaves	Total Inhabitants
1779	614	3,191
1802	669	4,567
1828	2,373	7,974

The 1822 conspiracy in Guayama

On the afternoon of the last Sunday of the month of September 1822, Juan Bautista Texidor, a slave of Jacinto Texidor, a prominent hacendado from the district of Guayama, was working in his vegetable garden until it began to rain.[96] As his labors were interrupted, Juan Bautista left his *conuco* and returned to his *bohío*. Sometime later, he ran away from the hacienda to an unspecified location, where nonetheless he found liquor as he got drunk.[97] We cannot establish from the available documentation whether it was on this occasion that Juan Bautista heard of the plans for the Republic of Boricua conspiracy, which involved slaves and separatists and which was being organized both on and outside the island. Nor do we know whether the plans were communicated to Juan Bautista by a certain Romano, a mixed-race individual of Dutch nationality who lived in Guayama and who was given the task of spreading the word about the conspiracy there. He was also an ally of Duboy.

On the way back to his master's hacienda, Juan Bautista took the road from Los Algarrobos, where he met the slave Francisco Cubelo, who was known to him as he had formerly lived in the house of his master Texidor. Francisco Cubelo had left his hacienda that afternoon with a note of sale stating that he could be bought for 325 *pesos fuertes*.[98] As he did not find a buyer, he was on his way back when he met Juan Bautista.

It was at that moment, therefore, that Juan Bautista invited his former workmate to take part in a revolution against the whites. The plans of the conspiracy were as follows: on September 29, the eve of the St Michael's night festivities—a holy day for the slaves—they would gather at the hacienda of his master Juan Texidor. The revolution of blacks would begin there and all the whites would be killed.[99]

Cubelo agreed to take part. The conspirators said goodbye to each other and returned to their respective haciendas. He had not managed to find a new master but now Cubelo had the dream of gaining his freedom in the near future. He was a slave with unusual qualities. Born in Costa Firme, he spoke Spanish, was married and over fifty years of age and worked in the fields. Lapre, his master, described him as very hardworking, very industrious and a good man whose only fault was that he was a bit talkative.[100]

The Sunday night went by and on the Monday, Cubelo and another two of Lapre's slaves were sent to harvest coffee. These were Mauricio and Gustavo, who were of French descent. At the coffee plantation, profiting from the security and seclusion of the setting, Cubelo invited them to take part in the Revolution, telling them that they must join it; that they should kill their master, his wife and children.

They should then go into town on the eve of the feast of St Michael because a Revolution was being planned against the masters.[101] The ultimate goal was to end up being the rulers of the country.[102]

Mauricio responded to Cubelo's invitation by saying that he was a black Frenchman, an honest man who could contribute nothing nor did he wish to act against the whites in any way. Gustavo pretended not to understand, claiming that he did not speak Spanish very well.[103] However, they understood the most important part, because once they were on their way back to the hacienda, the French blacks went to where Lapre was and informed him of the plans and the instigators of the conspiracy being organized in the vicinity of his own hacienda.

Lapre immediately seized his slave Cubelo, placing him in shackles and proceeded to look into the matter. Hours later, he handed Cubelo over to the authorities. At first there was confusion as to how many slaves had been plotting and who they might be, but the main ringleaders were soon arrested and sent to the local military authorities. Although a revolution did not break out, Pedro Básquez described the situation in Guayama on September 21 as extremely dangerous. He stated urgently in a letter to the Governor that, as they were surrounded by innumerable Africans and foreigners, their lives and freedom were completely threatened at that moment.[104] He urged him to establish whether this conspiracy in Guayama was connected to that of Pedro Dubois and Pablo Binet, who had already been arrested in Naguabo.[105]

Básquez also pointed out that, on the same day, the finest and strongest Spanish forces had assembled on the Guayama coast to prevent the disembarkation of an insurgent privateer that was said to have been maneuvering and attempting to land that night and the following morning.[106]

The conspiracy of San Miguel did not break out and the privateer did not land on the Guayama coast. Over the days that followed, from the 25th to the 30th September, they began to investigate the conspiracy. On the latter date a Court-Martial was held in the Casa del Rey of the town of Guayama. The Court-Martial was presided over by the Captain of the Militias, Vicente Andino and was composed of five judges. On orders from Governor de la Torre, Lieutenant Idelfonso Vasallo of the Regimiento de Granada acted as *fiscal*. The slaves were charged with conspiring against the whites.

Don José Colón conducted the defense of the accused. He based it on the fact that the conspirators were poor wretches who had been led astray by some people who had made the prospect of freedom ring in their foolish ears.[107] He also pointed out that they had not been aware of the significance and the seriousness of what they were supposed to do. He then asked that the death sentence be commuted.[108]

Despite the fact that both slaves admitted their offense, Juan Bautista alleged that, although it was true that he met Cubelo on the road from Algarrobos, he did not remember saying anything to him as he was completely drunk. During the trial Cubelo insisted that it was at that moment when Juan Bautista invited him to take part in the conspiracy.[109] In the closing stages of the proceedings, the *fiscal* asked Cubelo if he realized that the death penalty was applied to blacks who tried to make an attempt on the lives of whites. Cubelo replied that he did indeed know. The judge then pronounced the sentence and gave them the death penalty.

A few hours went by and at five in the afternoon they were taken to the marketplace of the district of Guayama, and, surrounded by the troops of the Regimiento de Granada, the Governor of Puerto Rico, Miguel de la Torre and other officials, the sentence was read out to them. They were made to kneel and were executed.[110] On the same day the bodies were taken to the cemetery to be buried by the parish priest and the mayor of Guayama.[111]

The proceedings of the Court Martial held in Guayama raise more doubts about the slaves' motives than they help to resolve. One of the most important issues is the lack of evidence in the guilty parties' confession and the informers' statement that this conspiracy was part of Holstein's expedition, which was to declare white independence in Puerto Rico. Although the authorities suggested it was the case, and the defense lawyer José Colón pointed out that these slaves had been led astray by people who had promised them their freedom, the slaves' statements did not link their conspiracy to the other one. These matters need to be investigated in other pieces of research, since Holstein never showed himself in favor of abolishing slavery. In fact, in Article III of "The Proclamation of the Inhabitants of Puerto Rico," he indicated that slavery would not be abolished as this would ruin the country.[112]

The prompt execution of Juan Bautista and Cubelo was not sufficient to set the minds of the white inhabitants and officers of the district of Guayama at rest. At the town council meeting of September 30, Alcalde Marcelino Cintrón asked the *hacendados* to present a list of their slaves, detailing their conduct.[113] He prohibited gatherings of slaves from one or more haciendas. Finally, he ordered that a white man be put in charge of every forty slaves.[114] These white warders should never let their slaves out of their sight, thus preventing conspiracies from being planned.

The conspiracy in Naguabo

In the district of Naguabo, in the Daguabo quarter, several slaves from the haciendas of Montiel, Crooft and Velo were plotting to kill their masters and all whites. This was what was reported by the mulatto, Juan José, a slave of Guillermo Crooft.[115] The military commander of the east went to the Quebrada Palmas hacienda and searched every shack without finding any conspirators.[116] The main instigator was said to be Duboy, a French mulatto from the town, for whom they searched diligently.

Meanwhile, the conspirators continued seeking out new converts for their revolutionary ends. On September 13, it was discovered that Duboy had traveled from Naguabo to the neighboring district of Fajardo, where he shared the plans with Saint Maurice, a French sugar planter. He reported the conspiracy to José Barceló, the Administrador de la Aduana of Fajardo and to a merchant named Tomás Rivera, as well as to Santiago.[117] They alerted the authorities, who duly proceeded to investigate the matter. Days later, Romano was captured in Fajardo and Duboy in Naguabo. They were both executed following a Court-Martial in the capital on October 12, 1822.

Finally, in Luquillo the alcalde reported that Petrona, a black woman from the district of Loiza who sold tortillas, was spreading the rumor that slaves would be granted their freedom on St Michael's Day.[118] As with the news of the conspiracy in Guayama, it was pointed out that if the slaves were not granted their freedom on that day, the whites would be massacred on St Michael's Day. Petrona was arrested and immediately sent to the capital to be sentenced.

While these events were taking place in Guayama, Naguabo and Fajardo, Holstein's expedition, organized over several months in the cities of Boston, New York, and Philadelphia and in New Jersey, set sail for the eastern part of the island. The expedition, which was backed by North American capital, consisted of 500 men, several schooners and arms and munitions.[119] On the voyage to the island of St Bartholemew, where they were due to meet up with those arriving from elsewhere, they were separated either by a storm or pursuit by a French sloop. Holstein's schooner was carrying 70 feet of water when it arrived in Curaçao.[120] There, the Dutch Colonial Governor impounded the schooners and arrested the conspirators.[121] In this way the conspiracy was crushed without firing a single cannon.

From the Bomba Dance
in Ponce to the
New Reglamento de Esclavos
de Puerto Rico of 1826

The canefields of the district of Ponce were the setting for the largest number of Puerto Rican slave uprisings and conspiracies during the nineteenth century. Five of the twenty-two slave conspiracies on the island between 1795 and 1848 took place at haciendas in Ponce. These were the most well-organized conspiracies, involved the largest number of slaves, and were, by far, the ones that presented the most serious and dangerous predicaments for the state. The first one occurred in July 1826, the precise moment when expansion of the Ponce canefields had reached its peak. During the 1830s there were five conspiracies. These were relatively unimportant but they paved the way for the large-scale conspiracy in December 1841. The last slave conspiracy there took place in 1848.

Baile de Bomba: conspiracy dance

Ponce became the main sugar region of Puerto Rico during the first half of the nineteenth century. On account of its economic and social prosperity it was equipped as the principal port in 1804. In 1816 it became the capital of the government district, and in 1821, the seat of the Military Command for southern Puerto Rico.[122] The land in the south of the island, and in particular that around Ponce, was the most suitable for growing sugar cane and was quickly acquired by the haciendas. In 1812, 240 acres were given over to cane. Between 1812 and 1821, a period of nine years, the number of acres almost tripled, from 240 to 690. Over the next five years, the rate of cane cultivation gathered momentum, with the number of acres tripling again, from 690 in 1812 to 2,070 in 1826.[123] However, this process of expansion in the first half of the nineteenth century was affected by the droughts that continually threatened the cultivation of cane and other lesser crops.[124] Although the agricultural techniques used were relatively modern, the irrigation facilities were limited, possibly because there were no major rivers. Another natural disaster that adversely affected the economy in the south was the cyclones and hurricanes that regularly lashed the coasts in this latitude causing devastation.[125] From 1813 to 1825, there were three cyclones and four hurricanes. These caused a huge amount of damage and did not help to alleviate the drought. The droughts and hurricanes undoubtedly exacerbated the poverty in which many of Ponce's inhabitants existed. Yet, as we have already seen, despite these natural disasters and the fires that regularly destroyed the canefields, cane cultivation was expanding. This was the environment that confronted the hundreds of bozal slaves who were forcibly brought to Ponce between 1815 and 1825. Despite the fact that the number of slaves there had increased at the end of the eighteenth century, from 354 in 1765 to 530 in 1776, it was not until 1821-1826, a period when the amount of acres sown with cane was rapidly increasing, that the numbers rose substantially. From 1812 to 1826,[126] the slave population increased to 3,204, as shown in Table IV.

TABLE IV
Free and Enslaved Inhabitants of Ponce (1765–1828)

Year	Whites	Blacks	Pardos/Morenos (Mixed Race)	Agregados (Laborers)	Slaves	Total
1765	—	—	—	—	354	3,314
1776	1,372	104	3,480	188	530	5,114
1812	3,221	—	—	308	1,000	9,838
1821	3,633	378	2,245	1,033	1,840	12,129
1826	4,326	—	5,910	1,487	3,204	14,379

Notes:
   Pardos/morenos were specialized terms often used in an arbitrary, self-serving manner by 19th-century Spanish colonial officials to refer to different gradations or preferences of mixed "black and white" persons.
   Agregados in 19th-century Puerto Rico was most often used to refer to landless rural individuals or families who found themselves to be perpetually in debt to the landowners whose lands they utilized for farming their own crops and growing cash crops for the landowners.

The amount of acres planted with sugarcane in Ponce rose more rapidly than the slave population, however. In 1812, there were five slaves per acre, whereas in 1826 there was just one per acre. Faced with this situation, the hacendados demanded greater output from their slaves.

During the period from 1815 to 1826 the District of Ponce received more than 323 emigrants. Favored by the privileges of the *cédula de gracia*, French, English, Italian and North Americans settled there. Some arrived in Puerto Rico with sufficient capital, technical know-how and foreign commercial relations to immediately establish sugar plantations. Within a few years, once they had become naturalized in Puerto Rico, these foreigners (now Spaniards) undoubtedly played a very important role, not only in Ponce's economic life, but through-out the entire island. The most distinguished emigrants who founded sugar plantations in Ponce in this century were Gregorio Medina, AM Archevald, Fernando Overman, David Laporte, Pablo Betiny, J Wedestein, and Oppenheimer, among others. It was also they who dominated political life in Ponce.

However, these emigrants also owned the *bozal* slaves who continually renounced the island's slavery system and its government. It was their slaves who were the main ringleaders of the most important conspiracies in Ponce and, in particular, the conspiracy of July 1826. The licenses for slave purchase in Ponce show that the owners of the conspirators had recently purchased *bozal* slaves. For example, Gregorio Medina, the wealthiest merchant in the town, and a landowner in the Bocachica barrio, had bought 153 slaves, 111 of whom were male and 42 women.[127] Fernando Overman, an immigrant and the owner of conspirators, had received licenses to import 200 *bozales*.[128] Another emigrant, Pablo Betiny, had bought 69 *bozal* slaves, 53 male and 16 female.[129] In sum, and as shown in Table V, all the landowners whose slaves took part in the July conspiracy had haciendas that had recently incorporated *bozales* into their workforce. Between them they owned over 752 bozal slaves who had recently arrived in Ponce. The *bozales*, having been free in Africa, were more rebellious than the naturalized slaves who had never known freedom. Subjected to slavery and a new work regime, the *bozales* began fighting for their freedom even while on board the slave ships at the coasts.

TABLE V
Owners of the Conspirators and Their Dealings in Slaves in Ponce (1826)

Name	Immigrant	Number of slaves imported in the previous four years	Male	Female
Gregorio Medina	YES	111	69	42
Pablo Betiny	YES	69	53	16
F. Overman	YES	73	46	27
J. M. Archebald	YES	88	64	24
J. M. Wedestein	YES	328	NO DATA	
J. Bautista	YES	13	5	8
D. Rodríguez	NO	10	6	4
J. Vargas	NO	35	25	10
E. Roque	NO	25	15	10
TOTAL		752	283	141

Source: Censo de octubre de 1826. Relación Nominal de Esclavos que tienen las haciendas en Ponce—18 de enero de 1827—Fondo de los Gobernadores, ANPR and Wedestein's license of May 1, 1825.

During the harvest of 1826, slaves and foremen at several of these immigrants' haciendas were planning a conspiracy.[130] The plan was carefully devised. They would start by setting fire to the canefields. This tactic was the main tool used by slaves in the Caribbean colonies before and after the Haitian Revolution. Northern Haiti was reduced to ashes after the Revolution. In the 1826 conspiracy in Ponce, the aim was not only to burn down a canefield but also that the fire would serve to distract and confuse the inhabitants of Ponce. They wanted them to believe it was simply another fire, like the many that had plagued Ponce in recent years and especially, that of November 20,

1820, which had razed two thirds of the town to the ground.[131] Therefore, with the conspiracy thus disguised, when the inhabitants arrived to put out the flames, they would not think that the catastrophe was the first stage of a slave uprising. The fire would be started in a canefield in the barrios of Capitanejo and Bocachica, near to the town. As the canefields were so close to town, it was expected that the fire would spread there, giving rise to a state of emergency among all the inhabitants of the district. When the townsfolk went to the canefield, the local garrison would be deserted, allowing some slaves to seize the arms stored in the Casa del Rey. According to the military report they would then proceed to kill all the whites. They would also loot the stores and, with the help of some of the overseers, free the slaves who were shut up in the barracks of the haciendas.

These rumors of conspiracy spread thoughout Ponce. Some slaves, such as Antonio Congo, a messenger and oxherd at the hacienda of Fernando Overman in the barrio of Aguas Prietas, used the freedom of movement which they enjoyed as privileged slaves to spread the plans among the enslaved population. The uprising was to begin on July 10, when Overman's slaves asked their master for permission to hold a bomba dance, as was customary on feastdays and Sundays. The dancing and the drumming inspired a sense of unity among the slave population. However, the dance was only a front for the slaves' subversive aims. Although the dance took place, the uprising had to be postponed until the following night as very few slaves turned up at the party.[132] On the following morning Oguis, a slave of Overman, went to the San Pedro hacienda, which belonged to Pablo Betiny, to spread the plans. Overman's messenger Antonio disclosed the plans to four slaves of Don Dámaso Rodríguez, the hacendado and alcalde of the barrio of Aguas Prietas in Ponce. However, José María, Celestino, José and León, who were slaves of Rodríguez, instead of following Antonio, hastened to tell their master of the plans of the conspiracy. He immediately alerted the military authorities so that they could arrest Antonio.[133] When he was captured, he incriminated other slaves and barely a few hours later over thirty slaves from different haciendas in Ponce had been arrested. We do not know how or under what conditions Antonio incriminated so many slaves nor how the local authorities, assisted by a regiment of grenadiers, managed to obtain full details of the conspiracy, and in particular, how they reached the conclusion that those arrested were the conspirators. Was Antonio's declaration the only one or had other slaves incriminated their comrades in rebellion?

Those arrested were tried by a military court, which ended on August 28, 1826. The following were given the death sentence: Benito and Oguis (owned by Overman); José, Félix and Ubaldito (owned by Vargas); Faustino and Federico (owned by Del Quemado); Manuel (owned by Esteban Roque); Pablo Viejo, Felipe, Francisco Antonio, Inés, Francisco, Antonio Congo and Manuel (owned by Gregorio Medina); Luis, Pedro Congo, Silvestre, Felipe, Salvador, Faustino, Nicolás (owned by Pablo Betiny) and José (owned by José Wedestein).[134] All of them were executed except for Ubaldito, Felipe and Manuel, who were granted clemency and had their sentence commuted to ten years' labor at the naval dockyards in Havana. This was because they were followers rather than leaders. The slaves Balthazar, Ambrosia, Baha, Cuacua, Ubaldo Luciano and Esperanza were sentenced to life imprisonment.[135]

The authorities obliged sixteen slaves from each hacienda in Ponce to attend the execution, in order to teach the survivors a lesson. Miguel de la Torre, the Governor of Puerto Rico, traveled to Ponce and was also present at the execution. The informants were rewarded with twenty-five pesos.

The Reglamento de Esclavos de Puerto Rico, 1826

The slave conspiracies in Bayamón in 1821 and in Guayama and Naguabo in 1822, the numerous escapes and attempted escapes by slaves and, in particular, the July 1826 conspiracy in Ponce, induced the Governor to issue a new set of regulations to govern the lives of slaves in Puerto Rico. The 1826 Reglamento [Regulations] was preceded by the *Real Cédula de su majestad sobre la educación, trato y ocupaciones de los esclavos en todos sus dominios e Islas Filipinas, 1789*

[His Majesty's Charter on the education, treatment and occupations of the slaves in all his dominions and the Philippine Islands].[136] Although both covered a number of similar aspects, there are three main differences between them. Firstly, the 1789 Code, which was issued by the King of Spain, applied to all his colonies. The 1826 Reglamento, on the other hand, was not issued by the King of Spain, as in 1789, but by Governor Miguel de la Torre. Nor did it apply to all the American colonies but only to Puerto Rico. The 1826 Reglamento emerged out of the experience of slavery on the island. Secondly, the 1789 Code does not specify who would be enforcing it, whereas the 1826 regulations indicated that the local judges of the district were responsible for its implementation. Thirdly, the 1789 Code professed to protect slaves from abuse by their masters, while the 1826 Reglamento claims to protect masters from the abuses of the slaves.[137] The main purpose of the 1826 Reglamento was to prevent conspiracies and to intimidate the slaves with potential punishments and other measures that would be taken against them if they rose up. The second part of the Reglamento, consisting of four chapters, was intended for this purpose. These measures had not been been specified in the 1789 Code. In order to prevent machetes being used as weapons in an uprising, Chapter V, Article I specified that all the haciendas should have a strong room with a good lock where work tools could be stored. The master or overseer was to be in sole charge of this room and this should not be entrusted to any slave. Similarly, Articles II and III detailed what was stated in Article I:

Art. 2. *"On leaving for work, each slave shall be given the tool he needs for his activity of the day, and it will be collected from him and returned to the storeroom when he has finished work."*[138]

Art. 3. *"The slave will never leave the hacienda with any work tool and much less with weapons of any kind, unless he is accompanying his master, the overseer or one of their families, in which case he can take his work machete."*[139]

To prevent the nighttime providing cover for conspirators, Chapter VIII regulated the times and places of rest for the slaves. Article III of the same Chapter regulated the behavior of the slaves within their rooms. There would be bright lighting during the entire night and one or two night watchmen would ensure they maintained silence. It was ordered that the slaves should stay quietly in their beds and that anything untoward be reported.

In order to prevent slaves from leaving their haciendas to disseminate plans for a conspiracy – as Antonio, a slave of Overman, had done in Ponce in 1826 – Chapter VI ordered the following:

Art. 1. *"No master or overseer of a hacienda will allow slaves belonging to another to visit; and when they need to go to another hacienda or leave their own they should carry a permit written by their own master or overseer, giving the day, month and year, stating the place they are heading for, and the period for which it is granted."*[140]

Article II, Chapter VI turned every inhabitant into a slave inspector, granting them permission to detain any found away from their hacienda.

Art. 2. *"The owners of haciendas and those who are not, white people and people of color, and even the slaves themselves, are authorized to detain any slave found away from the house and land of their master, to ask them for the written authorization that they should be carrying, and if they do not produce it, or if they have altered the course or direction of the place where they are heading, or if the period granted by it has expired, to arrest them and take them to the nearest hacienda (or to jail), where master or overseer will take the prisoner, secure him and immediately inform the slave's master, if he is from the same town, or the Alcalde, so that he may officially inform whomever it may concern, until they succeed in ensuring that the master has news of his runaway slave."*[141]

As the conspiracies in Bayamón in 1821, in Guayama and Naguabo in 1822, in Ponce in 1826 and the slave escape in Toa Baja in 1823 had all been planned during parties and *bomba* dances, Chapter VII regulated the slaves' recreations.

Art. 1. *"The masters will allow their slaves to amuse and entertain themselves decently on holidays, (after having heard mass and attended the explanation of Christian doctrine) on the estate, without joining together with those from other estates, and in a place open to the view of their masters, foremen and overseer."*[142]

Art. 2. *"These diversions and recreations will be enjoyed separately by the men in strength games such as singing, the balance beam, pelota, bowls; and the women apart from them in games of forfeits, picnics and other similar activities. Everyone, that is men and women, but separately, will hold their dances accompanied by the big bomba drums made of skin and other rattles used by the bozales, or by the guitars and vihuelas which the Creoles normally play."*[143]

Art. 3. *"These diversions will last from three in the afternoon until the sun sets or just after the call to prayer."*[144]

Art. 4. *"The masters and foremen are ordered to be especially vigilant that the the sexes do not mix, there is no excessive drinking, nor the entry of slaves from outside or of free people."*[145]

Finally, Article II, Chapter XI, of the 1826 Reglamento, relating to the freedom of slaves and the means of acquiring it, promised that any slave or slaves who denounced a conspiracy of slaves or of free persons would be given their freedom. In addition, the informer would receive a payment of 500 pesos. In cases where there were several informers this sum would be divided between them. Since the majority of the conspiracies were betrayed, this article appears to have been the most effective means of preventing slave uprisings in Puerto Rico.

Although the actual effects of this Reglamento still need to be studied, to these preventive measures were added others arising from the changing social and political situation of the European colonies in the Caribbean. For example, in the years that followed, one of the most common precautions was to prevent slaves from colonies where there had been slave revolts from entering the island. In 1834, slaves from all the Windward colonies were prohibited from entering as they may have been the cause of the disturbances experienced on the island.[146] The Reglamento, like other wide-ranging pre-emptive measures taken by Governor de la Torre and his successors, was accompanied by others for dealing with potential regional confrontations. These were issued by the Alcaldes and military leaders of each district. One example was when Alcalde of Coama in 1835 prohibited the import of Methodist bibles printed by the London Methodist Association. Alcalde Mayol said that the notes and expositions of the Holy Fathers had been removed from these bibles and the postulates had been modified and altered to propose absolute equality. This was directed in particular at the slaves and people of color.[147] The Alcalde added that these bibles had already been distributed in Kingston, Jamaica and the same was being planned for Cuba and Puerto Rico. The necessary steps would be taken to prevent the bibles from reaching the island.

Boom and Crisis in the Sugar Industry, 1790-1850

RAFFINERIE

Boom (1790-1840)

At the beginning of the nineteenth century, while the Latin American liberation armies were dismantling the Spanish Empire in America, the island of Puerto Rico enjoyed relative peace and political calm because its inhabitants remained loyal to Spain. Thoughout this turbulent period, the sugar industry proved to be the most important export line in the island's colonial economy. The international situation favored the expansion of sugar production as demand for the product was growing. The virtual disappearance of Haitian sugar created a huge shortage on the international market and the price rose from 4 *reales* an *arroba* in 1790 to 30 *reales* an arroba in 1800. The demand for the island's sugar also rose significantly on the United States market, where $12.72 per *quintal* was paid between 1800 and 1810 and $17.31 per *quintal* from 1810 to 1820. Similarly, in 1814 when the Napoleonic Wars ended, trade ties between Puerto Rico and Europe, which had been affected, were renewed. Sugar production undeniably became an extremely attractive venture for landowners in the loyal colony and for those foreigners who had settled there at the beginning of the century.

In 1815, in order to isolate the island from separatist influences and to encourage and develop the growth of commercial agriculture on a larger scale, the Gobierno de Ultramar issued the letter patent known as the *Cédula de Gracia*.[148] This abolished some import and export duties and taxes. It authorized the free entry of machinery, agricultural implements and slaves and also reciprocal trade between Puerto Rico and other foreign nations. The *Cédula* also promoted the immigration of foreigners to the island. It promised them land—680 hectares per white immigrant and 65 more for each slave they brought in—and exempted them from some taxes.[149] It also guaranteed them the right to become Spanish citizens.

The high prices, the incentives of the *cédula,* and the rising demand for Puerto Rican sugar all contributed to the large-scale development of the industry.[150] New haciendas were built, and between 1810 and 1842 production rose from 769,000 to 90 million pounds.[151] Table VI illustrates the increase in production around 1837.

TABLE VI
Sugar Production in Puerto Rico (1822–1874)

Year	Quantity in lbs.
1822	17,944,000
1838	45,664,422
1848	101,298,754
1858	123,542,292
1869	118,922,665
1874	184,577,204

The canefields moved away from the northern coast and were situated mainly in the virgin lands in the southeast of the island. The island's most important sugar plantations were developed on the southern coast, between the districts of Ponce and Guayama. The Irish traveler, George Flinter, on a visit to Puerto Rico during this boom period, described the southern area as lands renowned throughout the world for their fertility.[152] In 1841, the haciendas of Ponce and Guayama exported approximately 60 per cent of the total sugar produced on the island.[153]

By the middle of the century there were 789 sugarcane plantations in Puerto Rico.[154] The majority were small and medium-sized. The small plantations had an average of 20 to 40 slaves, the medium-sized ones had 40 to 90 slaves and the large ones had between 100 and 140 slaves.[155]

The first stage of the cane planting cycle normally began each year in the month of August when the most fertile lands, already cleared, were ploughed to make furrows. After ploughing, the prized seed was sown. One then had to wait for several months during which time the slaves occupied themselves by weeding the canefields, cleaning the sugar mill, cutting firewood and other preparations for cane-cutting. The harvest began in January. The duration of the harvest and cane crushing depended on the amount of *cuerdas* planted, the number of slaves, oxen and machinery available and other factors. The foremen woke the slaves at four in the morning. They then worked until nine, had a meal and returned to work cutting cane until nightfall. The canecutters, almost always the strongest slaves of both sexes, were each assigned a section of cane. Meanwhile, the cane gatherers— women and young men—loaded the carts. When the carts were full, they were taken to the crushing house or mill. The canecutting continued while the sugar was being crushed and processed.

During the first half of the nineteenth century most plantations used the primitive *trapiche de sangre* for crushing cane.[156] This was powered by oxen or slaves. There were also hydraulic mills and windmills. The quickest and most efficient were those powered by steam, but they were not very common on the island.[157] Once the cane had been crushed and the juice [*guarapo*] extracted, this was taken to the boiler house, where it was heated, boiled and evaporated to produce syrup. On account of the heat and the noise given off by these furnaces where the *guarapo* was heated, the boiling house was a place detested by slaves and day laborers alike.

According to the various levels of technical development, different grades of sugar were produced in the boiler house. The sugar most commonly produced in Puerto Rico during this period was muscovado rather than refined white sugar.

The sugar passed from the boilers to the curing house where the manufacturing and packing process was completed. From there the casks and crates left for the market.

Despite the fact that the majority of the slaves worked in the fields (rather than being domestic staff) as we have seen, both sexes were involved in the various tasks of cutting and crushing the cane. In addition to these tasks, some had more specialized jobs such as master sugarmen, oxen drivers, stokers, coppersmiths, cooks, sugar distributors, coopers, watchmen and even foremen. Therefore they did not all receive the same treatment, nor did they have the same living conditions.

The most privileged positions in plantation work were occupied by Creole slaves who were naturalized rather than by the African-born *bozales* who had been brought forcibly to the Americas. Despite the 1817 treaty abolishing the trade from Africa, a large number of Puerto Rican slaves during this period had been born there.[158] Their entry was facilitated by the active participation in the slave trade of the governors and other Spanish officers, by the contraband trade and bribes and other ways of flouting the law.[159] The number of slaves rose substantially during the first half of the century. Even so, the proportion of slaves to free inhabitants remained the same. In fact, in 1846, the year when there was the largest number of slaves on the island, around 51,265, their proportion in relation to free inhabitants was only 11%. The slavery means of production was never predominant on the island. Table VII shows the slave population of Puerto Rico during the nineteenth century.

The number of male slaves on the island was not very different to that of female slaves. For example, in 1830, out of a total of 34,374, 17,688 were men and 16,686 were women. At the beginning of the nineteenth century, the price of a male was higher than that of a woman, but as the price of all slaves rose and it became increasingly difficult to bring slaves from Africa, the price of women was higher. The enslaved woman suffered a double exploitation: work in the fields and sexual.

Although the price of slaves rose throughout the period in question, it is probable that the landowners continued to buy them because they preferred them to the free day laborers. The day laborers did not want to perform certain tasks on the plantations and they frequently abandoned the job. This was the view of the hacendado Juan Bautista Bertrés from the Cataño barrio in the District of Humacao. When he contacted the Governor in 1847 to ask for a license to buy slaves and bring them to the island, he argued that it was difficult to acquire them on the island and that he could not

TABLE VII
Free and Enslaved Inhabitants in Puerto Rico
(1812–1873)

Year	Total enslaved population	Total free population	Percentage of slaves
1812[1]	17,536	183,014	9%
1820[2]	21,730	230,622	10%
1830[3]	34,240	323,838	10%
1834[4]	41,818	358,836	11%
1846[5]	51,265	443,138	11%
1854[6]	46,918	492,452	10%
1860[7]	41,776	580,239	7%
1873[8]	30,014	617,328	5%

Sources:
1. AGPR. Fondo Documental de los Gobernadores, Censo y Riqueza. Censo de 1812. Caja 12.
2. George Flinter. *Examen del Estado Actual de los Esclavos de la Isla de Puerto Rico*, Instituto de Cultura Puertorriqueña: San Juan, Puerto Rico, 1976, p. 73.
3. Ibid., p. 73
4. George Turnbull, *Travels in the West Indies, Cuba and with Notices of Puerto Rico and the Slave Trade*. London: Longman, Orme, 1840, p. 555.
5. Rafael M Labra. *La esclavitud en el orden económico*. Madrid: Imprenta Nogueras, 1873, p. 242.
6. Censo clasificado de la Isla de Puerto Rico, 1854, ed. Cayetano Coll y Toste, in *Historia de la esclavitud en Puerto Rico*, compiled by Isabel Cuchi y Coll, Sociedad de Autores Puertorriqueños, San Juan, 1972.
7. Censo de Población 1860, in Francisco Pastrana, *Catecismo geográfico de la Isla de Puerto Rico*, Imprenta Marquez, Mayagüez, 1862.
8. AGPR. Fondo Documental de los Gobernadores, Censo de 1873. Gobierno General de Puerto Rico.

employ free laborers to cultivate cane because they generally did not want to work, and when they did, it was only for two, three or four days a week, or for enough time to satisfy their immediate needs.[160] Then they abandoned the jobs and did not return. Bertrés also said that there were hundreds of tasks on the plantations, such as that of the "*fondos*" [cauldrons] and that of the "*hornallas* [burners]", which the free laborers did not want to perform as the slaves did.[161] For all of these reasons—Bertrés concluded—he preferred slaves.[162]

This view was shared by Constantino Souteyran from Patillas, who asked to be allowed to import slaves, because one could not depend on the free workers as they abandoned the preparatory tasks for the harvests.[163] Souteyran went on to say that he had employed free laborers in the past and had experienced problems and losses.[164]

It is clear that the free laborers did not accept the working conditions on the plantations. In 1866, Leopoldo Krugg, the Vice-Consul of England in Mayagüez, one of the island's biggest sugar producing areas, confirmed what Bertrés and Souteyran had stated twenty years earlier. Krugg said that the free laborers only worked for two or three days a week, and only for ten or twelve hours a day, whereas the slaves' working day lasted for fourteen to sixteen hours. He also claimed that, as they had no other alternative, the slaves performed all the jobs ordered by the foreman, including that of the *hornallas*, since, if they did not, the whip would be used and they would be compelled to work.[165]

It is clear that the lack of confidence in free laborers should be regarded as an important factor in explaining why slaves were still being purchased right up until the moment of abolition, even though slave labor had ceased to be profitable for the landowners.

Crisis in the sugar industry (1840-1850)

This boom period of the sugar plantations in Puerto Rico was also characterized by several problems which, from 1840 onwards, prevented this industry from developing fully. The problems, briefly, were as follows:

Firstly, the price of sugar, which between 1800 and 1810 increased at the rate of $17.31 per *quintal*, and began to fall during the decade between 1810 and 1820 and maintained its decline. In the 1840s it reached the lowest price of its entire history, an average of $6.65 per *quintal*.[166]

Second, the demand for Puerto Rican sugar was limited because the market required a product of the highest quality and the island's plantations produced extremely poor quality sugar. The technological backwardness was evident, and the agricultural production costs were the highest in the Caribbean.[167] Meanwhile, beet sugar, with its lower production costs and better quality end product, was entering the world market.

Third, the United States of America, the main consumer of the island's sugar, began producing syrup from maple trees in the states of Vermont and New Hampshire. It also increased the production of cane sugar in New Orleans and Lousiana.[168]

Fourth, the high export tariffs stifled production and the tariffs were not adjusted in accordance with the drop in prices.[169] Faced with rising export tariffs, the United States retaliated against Puerto Rican exports.

Fifth, there was a critical shortage of ships in the island's ports. This gave rise to the undesirable situation of warehouses filled with sugar crates but with no means of exporting them abroad. If the production was transported in ships sailing under foreign flags higher tariffs had to be paid. The main consequence of this and the factors mentioned above was that the customers, which were, in order of importance, the United States, England and France, reduced their purchase of sugar from the island.[170]

Sixth, in 1834, the Ley Quinta, or Libro Quinto de las Leyes de Indias, which for three centuries had protected the sugar plantations from being seized by creditors, was abolished, leaving the hacendados at the mercy of the moneylenders,[171] who charged very high rates of interest. The situation was difficult, since the island was still experiencing a financial crisis. Also, the monetary reforms of the beginning of the century, like others implemented during these years including the decrees removing *macuquina* coinage from circulation, had been unsuccessful. Lacking credit, the island relied on foreign capital from friendly colonies such as the Danish colony of Saint Thomas.[172]

Seventh, the price of a slave had doubled and it became more difficult year after year to bring them to the island from Africa.[173] The free laborers could not be relied upon, as they refused to work on the plantations, abandoned the harvest, and frequently tended to run away. The system of servile labor was experiencing a real crisis.

Finally, there was the severe drought of 1839-1841, which affected southern Puerto Rico and destroyed the production of minor crops. Although it was slightly more resistant, the amount of sugar produced in 1840 fell.[174]

The economic problems facing the sugar industry in Puerto Rico affected the slaves as their masters felt obliged to demand greater productivity from them. Following a decade of relative calm on the plantations in the period between 1828 and 1840, the years of sugar boom prosperity, the era of greatest rebellion in the island's history of slavery was to begin.

CHAPTER
VII

Conspiracies on the South of the Island, 1830–1841, and the 1842 Conspiracy in Ponce

After the failed slave conspiracy of Ponce in July 1826, and following the enactment of the new Reglamento de Esclavos for Puerto Rico, the slaves never again seriously threatened the peace and political stability of the island as they had done between 1821 and 1826. Although there were six slave uprisings between 1826 and 1841, according to the local authorities of the districts these were isolated and insignificant incidents. Five conspiracies occurred in the south of the island, in the district of Ponce and its vicinity. [175] They all took place at a time when sugar production was rising rapidly and its export value was turning it into the most important item in Puerto Rico's international trade. Although the documentation is very limited, we do know that these were small-scale conspiracies, but they turned out to be important because they paved the way for the most significant slave conspiracy in Puerto Rico, which took place in December 1841.

Guayama (1828)

During the first half of the nineteenth century the Guayama district was one of the main sugar-producing areas of Puerto Rico. Hence it was a region where slave labor predominated. It was here that in 1822 Dubois and Binet, conspirators of the Docoudray Holstein expedition, were sowing their subversive seeds and succeeded in persuading some slaves to join them. The conspirators had attempted to involve the slaves in Guayama because they were the most vulnerable sector and liable to rise up in rebellion. The slaves plotted, but as in the case of Holstein's expedition, their attempt failed. However, they spread a great deal of terror and the governor, Miguel de la Torre, traveled to Guayama to attend the execution of the rebels. Six years passed uneventfully until December 15, 1828 when the slaves rose up once again. The primary sources for this uprising are limited. We know of only one document in the Archivo Municipal de Ponce which states that the authorities were alerted to what had happened in Guayama by means of a circular.[176] These circulars were sent out to the whole of Puerto Rico, warning the different authorities about the slave conspiracies, as well as other significant events. However, this uprising could not have been very important, as, if we compare this incident to the 1822 uprising in Guayama, the military response was minimal. De la Torre, who continued as governor in 1828, did not make an official visit to Guayama on that occasion, nor did he mobilize the grenadier regiment, or impose the death penalty on the conspirators as he had done six years previously.

Five years later, on January 21, 1833, there was a slave uprising at the Hacienda Los Pámpanos, this time in the neighboring district of Ponce.[177] The rebellion was suppressed and several of the offenders were immediately sent to jail. In order to pre-empt another uprising a company of patrolmen was ordered to police the area so as to maintain order in the town.[178]

Over the years that followed other incidents occurred, about which we have information that is not only limited but also contradictory. The first incident occurred on April 17, 1835, the date when the Alcalde of the district of Ponce was warned that a group of armed slaves, owned by Gregorio Medina, were intending to come to town to get Don Arturo Rogers out of jail.[179] Rogers was the co-owner of the Medina hacienda. Patrols were immediately dispersed through the town and those in charge of the rural barrios were ordered to patrol the region. Apparently there were no further incidents. Why did these slaves revolt? Was it really the case that this march was due to take place or was it simply an unfounded rumor? Why was Rogers, Medina's brother-in-law, in jail? Some issues still need to be clarified.

The third incident took place on the afternoon of October 2, 1835, also in the town of Ponce. On this occasion, when the inhabitants and hacendados were gathered to celebrate the publication of the Spanish Constitutional Code, it was observed that some slaves had arrived, separately and from different locations, at the shops in the town, asking for knives.[180] As the hacendados were absent from their rural properties, the military commander took precautionary measures in town and at the haciendas. Despite the fact that several conspiracies were organized for the precise moment when the inhabitants of different towns would be distracted, it is hard to believe that these slaves from Ponce, as the document states, would have gone in person to ask for knives. If this were so, they would have stolen them rather than asking for them. Besides, if the slaves were in fact away from their hacienda, this was in itself suspicious, since they were forbidden to leave the haciendas, as stipulated by the 1826 Reglamento. The military report stated that nothing had happened. Was this really the case? Was this similar to what occurred in Barranquitas in 1821?[181]

Finally, in the Barrio del Coto de Laureles in Ponce, slaves at the hacienda of José Arezany rose up on the night of August 16, 1839.[182] The uprising, however, did not take place at the hacienda of the landowner Roca, but at that owned by Juana Matos, which was in the same barrio as that of Roca. The slaves had been working there as hired labor for some time. Seven slaves were sent to jail. We do not know the immediate causes of this conspiracy but it is important to ask whether, under this type of arrangement whereby the slaves of one master worked for another master, the one who hired them was as much respected as their real master. Is it reasonable to suspect that the slaves, aware that Arezany was only a temporary master, therefore believed it would be easier to rebel? And finally, what were the terms under which they were loaned out?

The slave conspiracy in Guayanilla in the south of the island—the most significant in the series—marked the culmination of the resistence process in the 1830s. Guayanilla, to the west of Ponce, was one of the sixteen barrios of the District of Yauco. In 1833, its main urban center was a small town inhabited by ranchers and fishermen. The most important commercial product was sugar cane. In 1840, 2,970,413 pounds of sugar valued at 187,500 pesos were exported. There were 750 acres of cane under cultivation and three wooden and sixteen iron mills.[183] Compared to other sugar towns, Guayanilla was a medium-scale producer in Puerto Rico.

The drought in the south of the island adversely affected the small sugar haciendas and the small landowners who produced lesser crops in Guayanilla. This ongoing decline was the setting for the conspiracy of Guayanilla in September 1840.[184] According to Governor Méndez Vigo, the conspiracy aimed to set fire to the hacienda of one of the masters on a given night. When the inhabitants of Guayanilla went to put out the fire, the conspirators would then proceed to kill the whites and invade and loot the town. However, they knew that they had little chance of success in Puerto Rico, since once they had achieved these goals they planned to take possession of a schooner anchored in the bay and sail to the neighboring island of Santo Domingo.[185]

The conspiracy was uncovered on September 16, 1840. Initially 34 slaves were jailed who allegedly were directly implicated in it. They were tried and some were sentenced to be lashed by an executioner; others to a spell in the shackles. Two were handed over to their masters to be set to work on their haciendas under the necessary surveillance.[186] Another two, Carlos and Coutor, were moved to the prison in the capital. [187]

Despite the large number of conspirators jailed, the punishment was light because, according to the judges, the slaves had not discussed committing violence against the whites and they had not held meetings to formulate the plan.[188] Nor had they acquired weapons and the insurgents had not been assisted by people on or off the island. The governor concluded by pointing out that this incident had in no way affected the tranquility and calm of Puerto Rico.[189]

Despite such a satisfactory outcome for the authorities, on October 28, 1841, López de Baño ordered the military commanders of the district to provide three-monthly reports on foreigners and slaves. He also asked them to keep an eye on the slaves and ensure that they complied with the Reglamento of 1826.[190] He also emphasized the danger represented by emancipated blacks from other islands, and especially those from the American continent where free people of color had the same status as the whites,[191] and also the danger of the island's proximity to Santo Domingo, the scene of so many disturbances. Finally, he reaffirmed that it was the duty of the military to keep the slaves in check, and that if they did rebel it would be necessary to contain them, using—as demanded by any revolution—effective methods, the means for which only the military had at their disposal. [192]

It is evident that each one of these isolated and insignificant incidents raises numerous issues that still need clarification. These short-lived conspiracies also draw our attention to the fact that the information that we have about many of them is extremely confused. In addition, the initial reports tend to distort the events and almost always exaggerate what had taken place. This is later corrected by pointing out the unimportance of what had occurred. But these incidents also reveal that the authorities in the south were always aware of their slaves' situation and of the fact that they expressed, in different ways, their rejection of slavery. These events, and in particular the Guayanilla conspiracy, paved the way for the most important slave conspiracy in the history of Puerto Rican slavery: that of Ponce in 1841.[193]

The slave conspiracy in Ponce, 1841

Less than a year had gone by since the discovery of the conspiracy of September 16, 1840 in Guayanilla when the slaves of the neighboring district of Ponce began to plot once more. This was the fifth occasion in the preceding twenty years when the slaves of this district were planning a revolt.

In 1841, the year of these conspiracies, the sugar crisis in Puerto Rico escalated. Prices continued to fall rapidly while export tariffs remained very high. There was a shortage of ships for transporting the sugar, credit was becoming scarce, the price of slaves was rising and the technological backwardness prevented the manufacture of better quality sugar. In addition to these general conditions, which affected the majority of the island's plantations and slaves, a drought began in 1839 which mainly affected the south of the island. This, added to another series of problems, destroyed the cultivation of minor crops and resulted in huge losses on the sugar plantations.[194]

The planters found themselves obliged to reduce the funds set aside for the slaves' upkeep while also stepping up their exploitation in the canefields and machine houses. The slaves went hungry and, as the Alcalde of Guayama aptly observed during these years, "the man who is hungry is terrible."[195]

In response to the rumors of a revolt, the military authorities in Ponce ordered that the slaves be placed in barracks. Although it was prescribed by the 1826 Reglamento, placing the slaves this served not only to monitor them, but was also one of the worst punishments they could receive. Confining them to quarters proved ineffectual, however, because slaves from some of the haciendas of Ponce had been running away since October 1841 in order to plot.[196] The escapes were facilitated by some overseers at the estates who allowed the slaves to leave their haciendas at night. When the meetings ended, the conspirators returned to their quarters.

At one of these meetings, the slaves stated that they had the following grievances: firstly, they believed that they should be free, secondly, they did not accept the mistreatment by their masters, and thirdly, they were kept almost naked and were locked up in barracks.[197]

On another occasion in the month of October, a group of slaves met in a field of guinea grass at the El Quemado hacienda, property of Rabasa y Pedrosa in the Pueblo barrio. Although Rabasa had only eight slaves at his hacienda, the barrio was a strategic location because the largest number of slaves in Ponce lived there. In 1841, 910 slaves lived in the barrio, or a third of the total in Ponce.

At this meeting it was declared that Haiti, the first black Republic in the Americas, was ready to provide the Ponce conspirators with arms. According to the plans of the conspiracy, Jaime Bangua, a slave of Luis Font and the main leader of the plot, was planning to go to Haiti to seek the promised help after they had rebelled.[198] Aside from the Haitian support, the conspirators alleged that they had the support of members of the Sociedades Incendiarias and the Abolitionist Societies.

At another meeting held at the hacienda of Gerónimo Ortiz in

October—apparently the most important one—it was agreed that the revolt would be launched in the early morning.[199] However, at the same meeting it was decided that the date of the uprising should be changed to January 1, 1842.[200] Two members of the Secret Societies convincingly argued that on that particular day the town would be distracted by the present-giving during the New Year's festivities and, as was customary, there would be slaves in the town square dancing the *bomba* and celebrating alongside the free inhabitants of Ponce. According to the plans of the conspiracy, the uprising would not start in the plaza but in one of the canefields near the town at the hacienda of Inés Guillermety. A fire would be started there, the idea being to spread confusion among the inhabitants of Ponce. A group of slaves would hide on the road leading from the town to the canefield, which would be in flames, while others would seize the arms of the urban militia from the Casa del Rey located in the town.

Also present at these meetings were four Spaniards who were preprared to assist the slaves with the conspiracy. They supplied arms and also promised to make their own slaves rise up. Were these Spaniards members of the Abolitionist Societies or some other secret group? We do not have any evidence to indicate who they were, but we believe that their involvement in the conspiracy was crucial for two reasons: they persuaded the slaves to postpone the uprising for almost four months, that is until January 1, 1842, and they apparently also persuaded them to kill only the English and French masters.[201] Why not the Spanish masters? Perhaps they were better masters than the foreigners, who were now naturalized Spaniards, or did they ally themselves with the slaves against the foreigners? In short, what were the real intentions of the Spaniards, and most of all, why did the slaves trust them? There are many points that still need clarification regarding this incident as well as others.

Another aspect which gave the slaves an incentive to fight was the presence of *bozales*. According to the slave Marcos, these "*cabezón* [pigheaded]" slaves were very strong and very bold. It was felt that, if they participated, the plans would not fail as had happened in previous years.[202] One of these was a slave of Luis Font called Jaime

Bangua. Font had a dubious reputation and was at the time a member of the Ponce town council and the owner of a sugar plantation in the district. [203] The other "cabezón" was Manuel, also known as Dan, a slave at the El Quemado hacienda in the Pueblo barrio, where the slaves held one of the October meetings. He named the leaders as Celestino, alias Sogui, a blacksmith on the beach at Ponce; Goa, a Congo slave belonging to Gerónimo Ortiz, who was said to be a friend of Jaime Bangua from Africa; Alejandro, a slave of José Castaño; and Miguel, belonging to Esteban Roca, among others. Apart from the incentive of becoming leaders, they were also motivated by something that was mentioned at one of the meetings: "if there were so many blacks on the island then they could manage to capture it". [204]

There was a long period of waiting before the uprising: from October to January. During this time, the conspirators continued to meet on several occasions to discuss their plans. One night they met at the hacienda of Gerónimo Ortiz, where Goa, one of the leaders, was from. They decided to begin the rebellion on the following day. However, seeing that number present was very few, they decided to wait until January. [205] They needed to involve more slaves. In the days that followed, news of the conspiracy spread, almost always by means of the authorized activities in which slaves took part. For example, during *bombas* parties, which were very frequent, and at Sunday mass "they passed the word from one to the other". [206] Some took advantage of the privileges granted to them by their masters and the contact with other slaves who had permission to leave their haciendas.

On the morning of December 18, 1841, Isidoro, a slave of David Laporte, a Ponce landowner, was sent to Juana Díaz to take some piglets to a neighbour in that district. [207] On the way, he availed himself of the opportunity to share the plans with other slaves. When he reached the hacienda of Francisco María Tristany, Isidoro saw a group digging a ditch at the side of the road. Although he did not know these slaves personally, he approached them and shared the plans of the conspiracy, mainly with Marcos, Tristany's godson. Isidoro told Marcos that Thelemaco, a slave of Juan Castaño, had informed him that it was agreed that the conspiracy would begin on January 1, and that all the inhabitants of the region already knew of the plans and were quite prepared for it.

Marcos told his master of the seditious plans of which Isidoro had recently informed him. He betrayed the conspiracy in this way because his "master was very good and he loves him very much and had no complaints about any white person and respects them all".[208]

Tristany immediately informed Don Rafael de Sevilla, the first adjutant of the fifth battalion of the militia, who in turn proceeded to launch an investigation and take serious pre-emptive measures against the conspirators. With all the regional authorities alerted by December 21, Rafael de Sevilla ordered that immediate safeguards be implemented diligently and tirelessly, and that they should monitor the behaviour of the foreigners.[209] He also asked that a strong house or fortifications be built in Ponce and in Mayagüez, where there were many slaves who were concentrated on its large haciendas.[210] Meanwhile, according to Governor Méndez Vigo, this situation was arousing fear in the inhabitants. While the Ponce conspiracy was under investigation, the Governor linked it to an incident that had occurred a short while before in Toa Baja, where the slaves were apparently being incited to large-scale rebellion.[211] Which incident was the Governor referring to? Another conspiracy or revolt? Perhaps to the subversive lampoons inciting the slaves to rise up that had been discovered in that district? What link was there between the two movements? How was news sent from Toa Baja? What purpose was served by the lampoons if the slaves were unable to read? Once again, all is not explained.

Méndez Vigo's position was not very favorable either since he learned that there were no warships in Puerto Rico, which made it impossible to move his troops.[212] As a result, the Governor ordered a battalion of the grenadier regiment, a company of the urban artillery, another cavalry company and the troops and officers of a Cuban warship commanded by Captain Ramón de Hacha to report to Ponce.[213] On December 27, when the slaves' liberation attempt had already failed, a rumor spread through the barrios of Canas and Pámpano in

Ponce stating that the King of Spain had issued the order that the blacks should work three days a week for their masters and that they could work for themselves on the other days.[214]

The trial began on December 24. Jaime Bangua, Manuel (alias Dan) and Ramón Monro went to jail. Although the ringleaders remained silent, some were made to talk and they in turn informed on other conspirators.

Jaime Bangua, "the main ringleader" did not wish to confess to anything. On December 29, he and others were taken to the hermitage of San Antonio in Ponce, where they were jailed and could be kept isolated from other slaves and from one another.[215] This was because the hermitage had wooden partitions as well as bright lighting, something that was necessary at nighttime.

During the first days of the New Year an "ordinary court martial" was held in Ponce. It was agreed that Jaime, Ramón, Manuel (alias Dan), Celestino, Alejandro, Miguel and Thelemaco should be sentenced to the capital punishment of *garrotte vil [public garrotting— death by strangulation]*. Another four conspirators were sentenced to ten years' imprisonment in the fortress, and two were given six years in prison. It was ordered that the remaining four be guarded by their masters. It was not possible to find the main ringleaders of the plan, whom it was understood were not only blacks but also included some whites. Other slaves were acquitted while the masters of the guilty parties were fined for negligence and lack of vigilance.[216] Marcos, "the informer," was given his freedom and also paid 500 pesos, as authorized by Article II, Chapter II of the Reglamento de Esclavos de Puerto Rico.

The execution was carried out on January 17 on the El Vigía hill in Ponce.[217] It was witnessed by the overseers and four slaves from each hacienda in the district so that they might learn a lesson.[218] Also present was the aforementioned corps of soldiers, while the warship "Marte" was anchored in the port. Moreover, although the conspiracy was crushed at the start, fishing boats or Haitian trading vessels were prohibited to approach the coast of Ponce.[219]

The effect of the execution carried out in front of a large number of slaves and their overseers was to inspire terror and engender a state of submission. Rafael de Sevilla summed up the events in a letter addressed to Governor Méndez Vigo and dated February 6, 1842, in which he observed that "the terror of which the slaves are possessed is evident; they dare not leave their respective haciendas nor come to the town and besides, precautions have been taken so that slaves may not come to the town without a permit."[220] The punishment, Sevilla continued, "will last them for a long time and thus they will not hatch another conspiracy, either by themselves or together with the enemies who surround them."[221]

De Sevilla ended his letter with several recommendations to Governor Méndez Vigo for ensuring the peace in Ponce. He requested that a cavalry of responsible and veteran men be formed, that a strong house be built in the mountains to defend them from enemies of this kind, and that a fort be erected on the beach to protect the merchants and for defense.[222]

We do not know whether Sevilla's recommendations were followed, but seven years later in August 1848, slaves from Ponce revolted once more, in circumstances very similar to those that had triggered the 1841 conspiracy.

CHAPTER VIII

The 1841 March of the Slaves for Chapter II, Article III of the Reglamento de Esclavos de Puerto Rico

On Friday, January 1, 1841, Tomás Pamias, owner of the La Esperanza hacienda in the district of Isabela, noticed that a black lad on foot and two other youths on horseback had broken some of the links in his fence and passed through to the other side, heading for the Camino Real.[223] He called Eduardo and ordered him to find the run-aways so that they could be punished with several lashes. According to Pamias, soon afterwards he noticed a large number of slaves, led by Yam the overseer, walking spread out along the Camino real. However, he did not punish them since the main leader was the overseer and "if he were punished the others would lose respect for him."[224] On Saturday night he warned them that they would have to work on Sunday morning as a punishment. The following day, he ordered them to clear up the pools of water in one of the canefields which had been flooded by a stream. Pamias made them think that this Sunday labor was a consequence of their offense since they would have been happier to receive 200 lashes than be forced to work on that day.[225]

After several hours of work, 36 of the 46 slaves on the staff ran away from the hacienda. Most of the slaves, both men and women, were carrying their hoes, work tools and, as evidence of a poor and inadequate diet, their pots of food.[226] They immediately headed for the town intending to complain about their master to the alcalde of Isabela. Their grievance was based on the fact that Pamias had violated the Reglamento de Esclavos, which exempted slaves from working on holidays.

Cesáreo Zeno, the captain of the milicias disciplinadas which had set out in the direction of the district of Arecibo, came upon the mutinous slaves. According to the captain, the slaves were proceeding in a very orderly fashion and in silence. Zeno asked them where they were heading and the leader, Yam the overseer, replied that they were going to town to complain to the alcalde.[227] The captain ordered them to return to their hacienda, but Yam the overseer directed them not to stop but to continue on their march. Without weapons, munitions or armaments, Zeno was powerless to stop them and had to be content with going to the La Esperanza hacienda to give Pamias the news. On arriving at the hacienda, Zeno met Pamias who was getting ready to go out and look for his slaves.

Meanwhile, the slaves continued their march to the town, where they hoped to find the alcalde. Since Juan Ramón Ramírez de Arellano, the alcalde in office was not in town at that time, the slaves had to present their grievances to Carlos Garabaín, the so-called Secretary of the town hall and a citizen of dubious repute.[228] The slaves immediately lodged their complaint. Garabaín ordered that the Reglamento de Esclavos be brought out to show that they were obliged to work at certain times during the holidays when the cane was being crushed.[229] Although the slaves remained silent, the secretary's arguments did not correspond to the facts, because these slaves had not been working at crushing cane but were being punished by Pamias for breaking the links in the fence at La Esperanza the previous Friday.

When Pamias arrived with Zeno, shouting was heard. Yam and his wife were the most severely disciplined. They were taken back to the hacienda tied up with a rope and held at spear point by a soldier.[230] Meanwhile, Pamias himself took the rest of the rebels away. According to a witness, on the following day, Monday 4, "a dreadful punishment was carried out at the hacienda of Pamias."[231] Not satisfied with the initial report, on January 29, Governor Méndez Vigo ordered that the facts be clarified since the slaves had not received a fair hearing before the Síndico Procurador de Esclavos of Isabela, nor the intervention of a proper judge, "and they were severely punished nonetheless."[232] The Governor also pointed out that he had news that Pamias did not ensure that his slaves observed the holy days of obligation. The governor recommended that his conduct or morality be investigated and also that of Garabaín the clerk. He also ordered that the extent of Garabaín's influence on public affairs be looked into, and whether he had overstepped the very narrow and clearly defined limits of the Secretario del Cabildo.[233] Finally, the governor pointed out that the slaves' intentions should also be examined, and they should be made to understand the respect and consideration they owed their masters and others whose orders they were under. Méndez Vigo recommended exemplary punishment for the offense committed and urged that action be taken as quickly as possible.

That is all the information we have about the 1841 march of the slaves of Isabela. We have not discovered the ulterior motives which induced the governor to call for an investigation. However, and by way of a hypothesis, we suggest the following reasons: the price of sugar continued to fall on the international market with adverse consequences for the welfare of the island's slave population. News had been received of conspiracies being planned by the societies for abolition and by the Sociedades Incendiarias. Four months earlier the authorities had uncovered a slave conspiracy in Guayanilla, which although it never materialized, aroused considerable fear since they believed it was part of a general conspiracy of all the slaves on the island. To this was added the fact that the decade from 1830 to 1840 was a critical one for slaveowners on the island because England had abolished slavery in its Caribbean colonies.

In addition to the reasons just mentioned, it appears that location is vitally important for appreciating the potential danger of this slave march. Isabela lay to the north of Mayagüez and Aguadilla, two important centers where slaves were concentrated. The authorities could not allow themselves the luxury of permitting other slaves, whatever their grievances, to escape from their haciendas and go and present their complaints before the alcalde of their district. In Isabela there were not many slaves and this march involved only 36, but if the same thing had happened in Mayagüez, and there had been 100 instead of 36, the situation would have been quite different. In fact, although thay they were technically different districts, the distance between them was minimal. What is more, when the authorities issued legislation on slavery, they did not do it by region but on a nationwide basis. For example, the 1826 Reglamento, despite having been issued after a wave of conspiracies, such as for example, that in Ponce in 1826, nevertheless applied to the whole island. Lastly, the west of Puerto Rico was always the focus of the greatest separatist activity.

When the case was reopened on February 26, over thirty witnesses were questioned. However, none of the accused slaves testified before the court. There was a general consensus among the witnesses as to how and when the march had taken place and the questioning was limited to the points previously raised by the governor in his letter, cited above. The statements of the alcalde Ramírez de Arellano, of Cesáreo Zeno, the captain of the milicias disciplinadas, and of twenty-one other different witnesses including landowners, merchants, farmers, a sacristan, officers and soldiers, were very similar. All the statements described Pamias as an excellent master and a loyal and faithful citizen. Everyone also agreed that on the day of the march the slaves had been given a fair hearing and that they were treated leniently and also that in no case had the punishments been excessively harsh.

One of the thirty witnesses was Tomás Pamias himself. His statement, as was to be expected, is extremely interesting and gives us information about his view of events. Pamias began by explaining that he had punished his slaves for having broken the fences and had taken the opportunity to put them to work on a Sunday because two streams had overflowed into the canefield. He defended himself for having punished them on that day for breaking the fence of the hacienda. Finally, Pamias agreed that he had not fulfilled the obligation to take the slaves to mass, except on Good Friday, but he apologized and justified his offense by giving different reasons. Let us quote him directly: "because there existed between him and the priest very great cause for resentment, he fears (Pamias) that the aforementioned priest, in whom he does not have the least confidence, may attempt to lead his slaves astray."[234] His defense continued: "nor is periodic attendance at mass by slaves on the haciendas common either here or in other parts of the whole island, because there are tasks that always arise on the haciendas and above all, the owners fear close contact between some slaves and others, since from experience this leads to a thousand quarrels and disagreements that are injurious to the owners."[235]

Nevertheless, the statements of another four witnesses—and especially that of the parish priest of the town of Isabela—are very different from those of Pamias. These new statements completely undermined the image that Pamias tried to project of excellent master and good citizen, making it clear, on the other hand, that the whole population of Isabela knew about the ill-treatment he meted out to his slaves. It was mentioned that he always forced them to work on holidays. The statements revealed that Pamias did not follow the basic guidelines of the 1826 Reglamento. Anselmo Mareu, a merchant in Isabela, testified that when he had been in the Puerto de Pastillo five or six years earlier, he was watching Pamias' slaves carrying hogsheads of sugar when they were brought food from the hacienda. He noticed that they put the food in their mouths and immediately threw it up. "Getting closer, stated Mateu, he saw that the meal was beans and rice with so many little stones in it that obviously they could not eat it."[236]

The statement of Andrés Avellino Román, the parish priest of Isabela, was the most critical of Pamias. One of the most notable points in his statement was when he mentioned that Pamias, who had been living in Isabela for over twelve years, had never taken his slaves to mass, nor to confession, nor to any public religious ceremony; and, what is more, several adults who died at the hacienda had been baptized by a black man named Antonio Capataz.[237] In other words, Capataz was acting as the priest of the hacienda. He also pointed out that Pamias' behavior was "the most sinful that he has seen, because in the twelve or thirteen years that he has been living there he has always appeared to be a complete atheist."[238]

The slaves were not present when the inquiry statements were being heard. Therefore, after Avelino Román had finished his statement, José Estevan the *fiscal* visited Pamias' hacienda. There he observed, as he himself relates, that all the slaves were in good health, with none in the infirmary. Both the men and the women were robust and in splendid condition, and all were dressed with the proper decency and their clothing was in good condition.[239] In addition they had a spare change of underwear. The prosecutor also made it known that he had asked the slaves if they were happy and whether they had any complaints, to which some responded silently, and others in words, that they were well. As there were no complaints he proceeded to bring his visit to an end, exhorting the slaves to continue obeying well, without deviating from the orders and rules set by their master. He reminded them of "their duties and advised them that if they committed an offense, it was not only the master who had the power to correct them, the government itself would also punish them as an example."[240] Then, and although he had not done so throughout the entire visit, he asked the slave Eduardo, "the most ladino of all of them," to explain everything he had said to those who might not have understood properly. Why did the prosecutor concern himself at the last minute as to whether they had understood him, if he had not done so previously when he inquired if they had any complaints? On that occasion, as we already pointed out, the prosecutor seemed to interpret silence as indicating a lack of grievances. What atmosphere prevailed during that visit? Would the slaves have dared to complain again since they had been punished after making the previous complaint?

In spite of the fact that, as the prosecutor points out, most of the witnesses were men of the highest integrity, they were on Pamias' side. Also, although some of the statements are very serious, and Avelino Román, his harshest critic, considered Pamias to be a virtual dictator, he only received a fifty-peso fine from the judge for violating the Reglamento de Esclavos. All of this indicates the controlling nature of the priest, who, as the prosecutor pointed out in his final report, did not permit any course than was not of his will."[241]

We suspect that the information received by Governor Méndez Vigo about this incident and which prompted this investigation was provided by the parish priest. There is clearly a great deal of similarity between what the governor asked to be investigated and the most salient points of the parish priest's brief statement.

Months later, the decision to fine Pamias was commented on by Anacleto Bulta, a government officer, in the following manner: "It is to be disregarded that a fine of 50 pesos was imposed on Pamias for violating the Slave Code."[242] Furthermore, and referring to Avelino

Román, "it might be advisable to make him understand that his conduct is not that befitting his status, which demands complete with-
drawal from temporal matters," and concludes by saying that "if he
continues to intervene in affairs outside of his status and ministry,
measures will be taken that will result in his being corrected."[243]

CHAPTER
IX

The Capture of the Town of Toa Baja, 1843

Already by the closing years of the eighteenth century, the district of
Toa Baja stood out as one of the most important sugar regions on the
island.[244] It had four large haciendas: La Santa Elena, which was
owned by Juan Rijus (Ríos?); Feduchi; El Plantaje, owned by the
Quinlans, who were Irish; and one belonging to Agustín Losua.[245] The
latter, which was called the Media Luna, was originally founded by
Ceferino Nevarez. Fray Iñigo Abbad described it as the hacienda
where the island's finest sugar and rum were manufactured. He attributed its prosperity to the owner's intelligence "or on account of the
superior quality of the land."[246] The illustrious friar, who was extremely knowledgeable about Puerto Rico, pointed out that, because
of its location, this hacienda benefited from having its own jetty for
loading its production on board ship.[247] This was possible because the
tide rose nearby, giving greater depth to the River Toa.[248] He also
observed this advantage at other haciendas, which could transport
along the river their sugar already packed in boxes, as well as large
barrels of rum. The finest sugar was destined for the major ports of
Spain and foreign nations.

In addition to those mentioned above, there were other smaller
haciendas that supplied sugar to the town and the capital city. The
development of sugar in Toa Baja escalated towards the end of the
century between 1790 and 1800 when there was a shortage on the
international market. Production in Toa Baja rose enormously between 1776 and 1812, from 680 to 4,801 *quintales*. In 1812, 863 barrels of rum were also manufactured and 200 *quintales* of *melao* [cane
syrup].[249] This was obviously a result of the increased number of *cuerda*s planted with cane: from 138 in 1776 to 255 in 1812,[250] and the corresponding increase in the number of slaves. According to the 1812
agricultural census, one hundred and forty landowners or 43 per cent
were cultivating cane and producing sugar, rum and cane syrup. The
most prominent landowners of the end of the eighteenth century dis-

appeared and a new group of hacendados developed the sugarmills. In 1812, the main producers were, in order of importance: Santiago Ríos, Juan Ramos, Pablo and Santiago Córdova, Francisco Nevárez, Fernando Dávila, Silvestre Román, Francisco Antonio Hernández, José Rodríguez, Francisco Salas and José García.[251]

These landowners were also prominent political figures in the district of Toa Baja. They were town councilors or members of the Junta de Visita. In one form or another, they occupied the government posts, either through elections held among themselves or by recommendations made to the Governor by members of their own class. The Town Council of 1813 was composed of Francisco Hernández as alcalde; Santiago de Córdova, José Narciso Salgado and Francisco Marrero as *regidores*; Francisco Salas, as S*índico Procurador*; and José María Ramírez, as *Caballero Regidor*.[252] All of them were important sugar hacendados.

In the years that followed, 1813-1818, sugar production in the district of Toa Baja maintained its upward course. "Cane was the most successful product."[253] Pedro Tomás de Córdova wrote in his *Memoria* that "the lands of this district are the most productive of the island and its lovely plains covered with sugarcane create immense wealth for the country, which increases enormously with the cultivation of this plant."[254] In fact, the number of *cuerda*s doubled, from around 255 planted in 1812 to 615 in 1828. In the latter year they managed to produce 6,228 quintales more sugar than in 1812 (see Table VIII).

There were 28 iron sugarmills, which gradually replaced the original wooden ones. According to Pedro Tomás de Córdova, it was mainly in Toa Baja that the island's highest quality sugar was being produced. His opinion concurred with that expressed earlier by Fray Iñigo. There were also eleven stills that distilled 78 hogsheads of rum per year.

At the end of the 1820s, the El Plantaje hacienda, situated in the barrio of Palo Seco, was the most prosperous. Its new owners, the Irishman Enrique Buist, and his brother Andrés, had turned El Plantaje into the most productive plantation. In fact, on account of

TABLE VIII
Cuerdas Planted with Sugar Cane and Sugar Production in Toa Baja (1776–1828)

Year	Cuerdas	Quintales
1776	138	690
1812	255	4,801
1828	615	11,029

Source: See note 249.
Notes:
   A *cuerda* is a unit of land measure that varied in size over time. It most closely approximates a cord. One cord equals 0.97 acre.
   A *quintale* is a unit of measure that also varied over time. It most closely approximates a hundred-weight, i.e., it is equal to 100 lbs.

his wealth, Enrique Buist was the main contributor to the Toa Baja treasury in 1829.[255] Next to El Plantaje in terms of production and value was the plantation located in the Mameyar barrio owned by José Canales, the alcalde between 1825 and 1826, and that of the heirs of Santiago Ríos.[256] Although the descendants of old families such as the Nevárez, Ríos and Dávila continued to run the plantations, we can see how recent arrivals such as Buist, Caravallos, Landrón and others were making their way in Toa Baja society. The Salgado, Córdova, Ramos, Román and other families had already sold their haciendas, or their production was not increasing at the rate of those mentioned above.

   Urban development in the district of Toa Baja or "village" was very limited. According to the 1824 urban census there were 16 houses and 14 *bohíos* in the town.[257] Only two of these houses were general stores, the rest were for habitation. The most important commercial center was still in the Palo Seco Barrio rather than the barrio where the town and administrative center of the district was located. There were two general stores in the "village" whereas the general stores of Ramón Quinlan, Lázaro Pérez, Simón Roquet, Josef

Nieves, and Francisco de los Santos had been established in Palo Seco.[258] The main merchant house in Toa Baja, owned by Juan Soler, was also located in the Palo Seco barrio.[259] He was also a prominent slave trader and the brother of two important landowners in this region: Ramón Soler and Pedro Soler. They were the owners of the Hacienda Santa Inés in Vega Baja and the San Pedro sugarmill in Toa Baja, respectively.

The lack of a prosperous commercial urban center in the town contrasted with the aforementioned prosperity from sugar in the district of Toa Baja. There are several reasons for this. First, the old town was sited beside the river and was therefore an area that was easily flooded. This did not encourage the establishment of shops there for fear that they would periodically lose their merchandise when the great floods arrived. Secondy, because the town of Palo Seco had a jetty, a corral for holding animals belonging to passersby, and a boarding house, it acted as the springboard for trade between the interior and the capital city and from there to the towns on the east of the island.[260] In fact, as a result of its large-scale development, the inhabitants of Palo Seco separated from Toa Baja in 1839 and established a town with its own independent administration.[261] Finally, as has been pointed out, since the main landowners lived in the urban zone of the capital city, from the time of colonization. They benefited from the richness of the Toa land while enjoying the profits in the capital.

It is precisely in the decade between 1830 and 1840 that we find a large number of haciendas whose owners resided in the capital and that were managed by residents of the district. The notarial records available for this period, 1836-1843, are full of certificates granting extensive powers of attorney to people in Toa Baja. For example, one of the cases in 1840 is that of Francisco Cantero, a merchant and resident of the capital who granted a general power of attorney to Juan Landrón to "engage in the administration of his sugar plantation in the Barrio Mameyal of Toa Baja."[262] Landrón was also able collect and pay debts, grant loans, argue lawsuits and sell land in the name of and as the representative of the owner. This made him the overall manager of the plantation, which was small, consisting of 40 *cuerdas* of land, twenty of which were planted with sugar cane, an iron mill, copper drums and armaments, and a distillery with four raised cauldrons. [263] There was also a house, a *rancho bagacero*, a corner plot planted with bananas, and several coffee bushes, as well as other items. The hacienda was worked by several slaves, some from the Longoba nation. In addition to acting as the general agent for Cantero's hacienda, Landrón was alcalde from 1842 to 1843, and was also involved in the running of one of the largest haciendas of Toa Baja: El Plantaje.

Over the following years, 1830-1846, the district of Toa Baja was supplanted as one of the most important centers of production. Sugar continued to be manufactured there but other districts such as Ponce, Guayama and Mayagüez became the island's main sugar-producing areas. Nevertheless, the number of *cuerda*s planted with cane in Toa Baja increased during this period, from 615 in 1828 to 1,004 in 1846. Twenty-five iron sugarmills were crushing cane at that time, and the heirs of Ríos, Canales, Marrero, Salgado, and Hernández continued to make up the dominant class of the district.

The separation of the town of Palo Seco, which, as mentioned earlier, occurred in 1839, implied the loss of the wealth represented by the El Plantaje hacienda and its public jetty. This represented a sudden and significant setback for the subsequent development of sugar in the district of Toa Baja. As it was, the foundation of the town of Dorado in the 1840s removed a large portion of its better land from Toa Baja, leaving only the barrios called Sabana Seca, Candelaria and Media Luna.[264] When this territorial break-up occurred, Toa Baja lost 12 of its most important sugar plantations.[265]

While this was happening, the sugar industry throughout the island was also experiencing its worst crisis of the nineteenth century. This was due to several factors, the most important being the fall in the price of sugar. In the 1840s, the *quintal* reached the lowest price in its history. The average price during that decade was $6.65 per *quintal* on the Philadelphia market, or, some $10.66 less than at the beginning of the century (1800-1810). Other factors were added to this terrible situation, such as the haciendas' technological backwardness, the high customs tariffs, the high price of slaves, the shortage of ships, the lack of credit and other factors which exacerbated the state of the colony's industry. The fact of the matter is that everything pointed to instability in the town. This affected all orders of Toa Baja society, including of course, the slaves living in the district.

From the time when the first sugarmills were established in Toa Baja, including that of the heirs of the family of Juan Ponce de León, the sugar industry had been closely linked to black Africans and their American descendants. As this industry began to develop on a large scale at the end of the eighteenth century and beginning of the nineteenth, the number of slaves almost doubled, from 208 in 1776 to 410 in 1827 (see Table IX).

TABLE IX
Population of the District of Toa Baja

Class	1776	1827	1846
Free	2,203	2,502	2,979
Enslaved	208	410	770

Despite the fact that the treaty for the Abolition of the Slave Trade, prohibiting Spanish and English merchants from trading in slaves from the African continent, was in force from 1817, most of the slaves in Toa Baja, in open violation of the spirit of the treaty, actually originated on the west coast of Africa, especially the region of the Congo.[266] For example, one of the most prosperous haciendas of the district, owned by the Frenchman José Marsan and situated in the Media Luna barrio, in 1839 had a staff consisting of forty-seven slaves, thirty-four of whom were in fact African-born.[267]

We do not have sufficient evidence to arrive at firm conclusions as to the extent of the slave trade in the capital city, where we believe people from Toa Baja bought most of their slaves, but we have examined the contracts of sale in Toa Baja using the notarial records for the years between 1836 and 1843.[268] This documentation gives us an idea of transactions in the locality. For this period, 73 slaves are listed as having been sold and we recall that in 1846 there were 770 slaves in Toa Baja. The documents only allow us to discover the sex of 58 slaves, 36 of whom were male and 22 female.

During the first decade of the nineteenth century, slaves in Toa Baja showed signs of constant resistence, expressed through frequent individual or collective escapes and conspiracies.[269] These signs of dissent paved the way for the great conspiracy of 1843.

Already in July 26, 1821, plans were being drawn up for the slave uprising in Bayamón. This involved conspirators from several haciendas in the neighboring district of Toa Baja.[270] Although the majority were from Bayamón, when the alcalde José Córdova heard the news in Toa Baja, he mustered all the military forces he could, ensuring that the hacendados made their domestic slaves hand over the tools required for their labours, and any other implements that could be offensive weapons. Although the Bayamón conspiracy was uncovered before anything could happen, six slaves belonging to Juan Ríos, a prominent hacendado from the Media Luna barrio of Toa Baja, were taken for questioning.[271] Another four slaves who were found away from their hacienda were arrested in Toa Baja.

Two years after the failure of the Bayamón conspiracy forty slaves from Toa Baja, profiting from the fact that the town was distracted by the Saint James festivities, escaped to the region of Guarico in Haiti.[272] Of the forty, twenty were from Juan Ríos' staff, seven were the property of José Canales, six belonged to Santiago Rapp, two to Luis Marrero and one to Juana López. The remaining four were owned by other hacendados in the district.[273]

On another occasion, in July 1826, slaves from several haciendas in Toa Baja and Bayamón joined forces to plan an escape to Haiti. The plot was disseminated among the slaves by means of a "bomba" sung by José Joaquín, slave of Miguel Dávila.[274] When he finished singing, he asked for money, a boat to escape to Haiti and merchandise, and invited others to flee with them.[275] Apparently another slave from the

El Plantaje hacienda, known as Tío Bautista, who belonged to the Irishman Enrique Buist, helped the conspirator to spread the seditious message. It was in fact a child slave of Enrique Buist who informed his master of the plans for escape, when he arrived at his hacienda El Plantaje on July 18. Buist, in turn, reported the escape to the authorities, and proceeded to take all possible steps to thwart the plan, which was not put into action.

The conspiracy of the Longoba

On the afternoon of Sunday March 26, 1843, a group of slaves of the Longoba nation were playing *bolas* [ninepins] at the hacienda of the absentee landowner and merchant, Francisco Cantero, which was situated in the Mameyal barrio of Toa Baja.[276] But apparently they did more than play, as it was there that a plan to seize the town was devised. That afternoon Cornelio, alias "Bembé," of the Longoba nation and the leader of the conspiracy, had complained to his fellow slaves that he was not given food at his master's hacienda.[277] The leader of the conspiracy was owned by Doña Concha Passalacqua, the widow of Juan Hernández, a Toa Baja family with a long tradition of producing sugar. Doña Concha's hacienda was situated to the east of the town, adjoining it, and was managed by Pascasio Charbonieu.[278]

When night fell, Bembé and another of Doña Concha's slaves ran away, along with Enrique Longobá, Casimiro, Eduardo, Luis, Pedro, Lucas and others from the Cantero hacienda. Their destination was the town, approximately a mile and a half from where they had gathered that afternoon. Before they reached the town, they hid in a ravine on the eastern bank of the River Toa. From there they crossed to the town square and captured the Casa del Rey without encountering much resistence.[279] In this building, the seat of the Ayuntamiento, the arms of the military garrison were kept, and hence the weapons and munitions of the Toa Baja Militia. They seized these, left the Casa del Rey and crossed the square once more heading for the bell tower of the church. The rebels intended to occupy the tower.

We strongly suspect that the slaves who had risen up in arms wanted to ring the bells as a perhaps pre-arranged signal to announce to other slaves in the district that the revolutionary movement had commenced with this initial victorious act.

But in fact, alerted by the capture of the Casa del Rey, the parish priest Domingo Villanueva and the Catalan resident merchant and hacendado Don Francisco Maymí were taking refuge in the church bell tower. Apparently the battle to capture the bell tower lasted so long that it allowed time for Rafael de Sevilla, the experienced Sargento Mayor of the Milicias Disciplinadas, to arrive, along with other inhabitants who were ready to confront the rebels and prevent them capturing the bell tower and the town.

After several hours of fighting, during which five soldiers and the ringleader Bembé were killed, the slaves were forced to withdraw from the town. By the early morning, thwarted in their attempt to control the bell tower, and in evident disarray, they sought refuge in the canefields near to the town.[280] Soldiers, alcaldes, urban militamen and inhabitants from Toa Baja and the neighboring towns, assisted by the first battalion of the Milicias Disciplinadas, which had arrived from Bayamón at seven in the morning, moved into position for attacking and capturing the insurgents. Also in the early morning, the Cazadores of the Compañía de Peninsulares de Guarnición arrived. All the soldiers and followers went to the canefield, from where most of the shots fired by the rebels were originating. The military captain ordered them to surrender but was not heeded. He then ordered that the canefield be surrounded, stationing men fifteen paces apart so as to cover the whole area.[281] As this did not immediately have the desired effect, they then proceeded to set fire to the canefield. This strategy was not successful either, because at eleven in the morning it started to rain and the fire was extinguished. When this failed, they let some bulldogs loose in the canefield so as to "flush out" the rebels. But this tactic was also unsuccessful. The slaves, positioned at the highest point in the canefield, had the advantage of being easily able to see the soldiers who were pursuing them. Eventually, each of the urban militamen was given a machete. They began to cut the cane and, covered by the arms of the Milicias Disciplinadas, they managed to reach the rebels and capture eight of the rebellious slaves.[282]

The pursuing force moved on from there to another canefield where more slaves had taken refuge and from where shots were emerging sporadically. This time they managed to set fire to the cane-field and another two slaves were taken prisoner. The Captain of the Militias then went with his armed force to another canefield on the opposite side from where the last operation had been conducted, and from where shots were also emerging. He employed the same tactics but did not find anyone.[283] Following this search and news that there were more rebellious slaves at the canefield on Doña Concha Passa-lacqua's hacienda, where Bembé came from, the captain conducted a reconnaissance of the area and concluded that the slaves of the dis-trict had been sufficiently frightened and that it was therefore not nec-essary to set fire to any more canefields. Nevertheless, he stationed patrolmen at the hacienda and other strategic points in the neighbor-hood.

Once the revolt had been suppressed those who had been arrested were tried in a military court. Sentence was pronounced on May 10, 1843. Eight slaves were executed in the presence of a group of slaves from Toa Baja who were taken to witness the act so that it would serve as a warning.[284]

The victory of the Milicias Disciplinadas, the Milicias Urbanas and the Cazadores was due, among other things, to their greater num-bers, military preparation and weaponry. The prompt mobilization of these forces from San Juan, Bayamón and other neighboring towns, was also a factor that influenced the outcome. However, we do not know exactly how many soldiers, officers or residents were mobilized during the period of the uprising. Although no one was able to give a precise answer to the captain of the militia when he asked how many insurgents there had been on the morning of March 27, those he asked estimated the number of rebels at around twenty slaves.[285]

News of the alarming slave uprising in Toa Baja spread through-out the entire island. In districts as far away from the scene of events such as Maunabo and Loíza, pre-emptive measures were taken and the authorities in those towns asked the Gobierno Superior to supply them with weapons for their defense in the event of something similar to what had happened in Toa Baja.[286] For example, in Loíza they asked for the unit of the military detachment to be increased to fifty soldiers because three quarters of the population were black, counting free men and slaves.[287]

In the days that followed the civilians and soldiers who had defended Toa Baja, as well as the relatives of those who died during the slave revolt, received decorations from the government. Domingo Villanueva, the parish priest who had defended the bell tower during the uprising was awarded the Cross of Isabella the Catholic. Juan Landrón, the alcalde of Toa Baja, who had defended the town on the night of the uprising, also received the Cross of Isabella the Catholic. The families of Francisco Gendo, José Achavales, José Ballet and Bruno Ortiz were also awarded the same decoration. The families of Miguel Martínez, Manuel Feliz and José María Fanfonario were given pensions of six pesos. Finally, Alonso Delgado, the sergeant of the three companies of Milicias Disciplinadas who took part in suppressing the uprising, was promoted to second lieutenant.[288]

We believe that the general causes of the uprising were linked to the widespread crisis in the island's sugar industry. As we have already indicated, the Puerto Rican sugar industry was confronting a number of problems in 1842. In particular, the price fell to $6.18 a *quintal*, well below the average price in the 1830s which had reached $18.48. The profits were lower and thus the funds for maintaining the slaves were reduced. There seem to have been several reasons behind the conspiracy. On the one hand, Bembé, the leader of the uprising, complained about the ill-treatment and inadequate nutrition he received at the hacienda of Doña Concha Passalacqua. But not all the insurgents were from the same hacienda. Why, then, did they take part? We suggest that one reason was the deep tribal unity of these slaves of the Longoba nation. They put the finishing touches to the details of their conspiracy at a "juego de bola" in the afternoon and that night they rebelled. The *bozales*, slaves brought directly from Africa, frequently proved to be more rebellious than those born in America. Their defiance and leadership of previous uprisings was acknowledged by the other slaves. It was precisely these circumstances: the tribal cohesion and the swift execution of the plans, that explain why this was the only slave uprising in Puerto Rico to succeed in its initial moments. In previous uprisings slaves had never managed to occupy the Casa del Rey and seize the weapons stored there.

CHAPTER
X

The Bando Contra la Raza Negra and the 1848 Slave Conspiracy in Ponce

Following the drought in southern Puerto Rico, which lasted from 1839 to 1844, the Ponce hacendados attempted to develop an irrigation system between 1844 and 1847. This would enable them to avoid financial ruin in the event of another drought. These hopes were short-lived because the rivers could not supply them with water.[289] Some hacendados, convinced that irrigation would guarantee the cane harvests, had appropriated the rivers, preventing other farmers and hacendados from using them. Others claimed that if part of a river flowed through their land, it therefore belonged to them.[290] According to David Laporte, the alcalde of Ponce and a hacendado, it rained at the beginning of the summer of 1844 and there were hopes of a better sugar harvest.[291] However, another drought began in November 1845 and lasted for the following two years, adversely affecting sugar production, which fell by 2,234,244 pounds.[292] It fell from 24,277,217 pounds in 1846 to 21,944,973 pounds in 1848. The drought also spoiled the harvest of lesser crops, severely affecting the general economy of the south of the island.[293]

Two months before the July 1848 slave conspiracy, the district of Ponce was in a sorry and impoverished state. As indicated earlier, the drought was the main cause. But there were other problems that were as serious as this disaster. The price per *quintal* of sugar had fallen to $5.14 on the Philadelphia market in the United States – the main customer for Ponce production. This was the lowest price paid in the nineteenth century.

The situation was exacerbated by the fact that the hacendados were unable to dispose of the sugar, not even if they sold it at the knock-down price of two pesos per *quintal*.[294] Another factor that did not improve matters was the need for ships to export sugar consignments. The warehouses were filled with sugar that had no outlet. Creditors, especially those from Saint Thomas, lost confidence in the Ponce hacendados. "Ruin was plain for many of them."[295] Some haciendas were put up for auction in order to force their owners to pay the local taxes or rates on their property.

Finally, the French market, the third most important customer for Puerto Rican production, stopped buying sugar as a result of the turbulent political events of 1848.[296] The French Revolution and the founding of the second republic in that year had another more direct effect on the lives of slaves of the Caribbean and hence on those in Puerto Rico. On April 29 the French provisional government abolished slavery in the colonies of Martinique and Guadeloupe. The slaves in Martinique did not wait for this decree but rose up. Many whites abandoned the island and fled to Puerto Rico.[297] When French people from the privileged classes arrived there, they described the horrors of the racial war they had just experienced. By July 3 the conflict had spread to the Danish colony of Saint Croix where the governor, hoping to appease the colored insurgents, abolished the institution of slavery. However, this measure failed since the war took its course.

The geographical proximity of the islands of Puerto Rico and Saint Croix and the ongoing economic crisis affecting both the sugar plantations and the slave population of Puerto Rico prompted Juan Prim, the governor of the island, to send a contingent of 500 infantrymen, two pieces of artillery and a unit of sappers to Saint Croix.[298] On this occasion Puerto Rican forces, along with the Danish ones, managed to restore peace in Saint Croix. However, Governor Prim feared that the slaves' belief that violence was the only means of abolishing slavery would be reaffirmed. He therefore found himself obliged to persuade the Danish authorities and even the slaves in Puerto Rico that the decree abolishing slavery in Saint Croix was a "dead letter" since it had been forced upon them. Prim indicated to the Danish authorities that they should not put this abolition decree into effect as it would set a bad example to the slaves of Puerto Rico.[299]

The second of Prim's measures came into force at the end of May 1848, when the governor launched an attack on the free blacks and slaves of Puerto Rico. On this occasion, he issued the Bando Contra La Raza Negra [Decree against the African Race].[300] This was a repressive and punitive decree that made no distinction between free Africans and slaves. It was enough merely to be African or a descendant of Africans to be included in the stipulations of the decree. According to Article I, any offense in which members of the African race, free or enslaved, were involved, would be tried and punished by a military court. Article II reaffirmed the superiority before the law of the white person over the black person when it pointed out that any African taking up arms against whites "even if the aggression were justified," would, if he were a slave, be executed and if a free person, would have his right hand cut off.[301] Africans and their descendants would always be guilty before the law. Article III made it clear that if a black person verbally insulted, roughly handled or threatened someone with a stick, stones, or in any other manner, he would be sentenced to six years in jail if he were a slave. If he were a free man he would be given a punishment corresponding to the circumstances surrounding the deed. Article V authorized masters to kill any slave who rose up in such an act.[302]

Seemingly the resolutions of the slave code were not clear, as nine days later Prim issued another explanatory decree to make it easier to implement the slave decree.[303] Article I extended the conditions stated in Articles II, II, and V of the Bando Negrero regarding the property of the whites. Any theft by Africans or their descendants would be dealt with by a court martial.[304] Articles VIII, IX, and X specified that if a slave stole eight *reales* he would be handed over to his master but if he stole between eight and eighty *reales* he would be given 200 lashes.[305] Anyone setting fire to a rural or urban farm, canefields or other cultivated fields would be judged by a court martial. Prim was also concerned about any fights that might break out between people of color, free or enslaved, and the punishments would correspond to the weapons used.

The conspiracy of Ponce, 1848

The Bando Negrero was greeted with approval in the district of Ponce. Here the concentration of slaves was higher than anywhere else on the island: 61.1 per cent of the total. It was also an area where their fighting spirit and rebelliousness had been a constant. After the previous conspiracy, uncovered on December 23, 1841, the slaves were subjected to brutal punishments and other preventive measures. These had demonstrated to the military commander, Rafael de Sevilla, that the punishments had been a good deterrent on that occasion (see the 1841 conspiracy). Over the following years the slaves were constantly reminded of the violence of which the authorities were capable. They were forced to witness the punishment and executions of rebellious slaves.[306] Similarly, between 1841 and 1848, other measures were taken to preempt situations that could enable the Ponce slaves to rebel, as, for example, in July 1845, when it was suggested that it was dangerous for the slaves to have taverns near to the fields at the haciendas.[307]

Again, in July 1848, in the midst of the sugar harvest, events in Martinique, Guadeloupe, and Saint Croix, and the repression resulting from the Bando Negrero, David Laporte, the alcalde of Ponce, was anticipating further rebellious outbreaks by the slaves. In official letter number 19 dated July 11 (four days before the conspiracy was uncovered), he ordered all hacendados that on no account should they put their slaves on guard duty in their sugarmills at night as they had hitherto been accustomed to doing.[308] The alcalde went on to say that they should be replaced by a hundred white men who would be extremely useful in the light of events. Finally, he justified his decree by saying that it was needed to maintain the peace.[309] Laporte was well aware of the background to the Ponce slave rebellion. Isidoro, one of the slaves who led the rebels in December 1841, belonged to him and in 1845 he had also indicated that the tavern on his hacienda represented a danger for the slave population.

These measures did not suffice because, four days later, Laporte once again needed to find a way to ensure peace in the town. On this occasion he asked Governor Prim for an infantry corps for his district.[310] Clearly, Alcalde Laporte suspected that some attempt at uprising was under way. His fears proved to be right. On July 15, a conspiracy was uncovered involving slaves from several haciendas in

Ponce. The names of the leaders were Agustín, alias Goleta, Nicolás, Pedro, Tomás, Damián, Pablo, Yambo, Enrique, and Cayetano.[311] According to the authorities, the plan for the uprising followed the classical pattern of slave revolts in Puerto Rico: set fire to the cane-fields, destroy the town, abolish slavery, and kill all the white inhabitants.[312] Similarly, the way in which the conspiracy was uncovered also followed the established pattern. Pablo Yambo, a slave of Tristany, informed Santiago, a slave owned by David Laporte, of the plans for the conspiracy and asked him to take part. He told him that he would return later with more information and that he would let them know when the conspiracy was due to start. Santiago immediately went to his master, David Laporte. He informed him about what had happened, pointed out the leaders and provided details of their plans. An infantry corps was sent immediately to Ponce and the militia arrested twelve slaves there and then. We do not know whether these slaves offered resistance or whether they were the ones mentioned by Santiago, or if there were others. Once the slaves had been subdued, Pablo Yambo and Francisco were executed following a military trial on July 20. The execution was witnessed by twelve slaves from each hacienda in the district of Ponce.[313] Five days later, Agustín, alias Goleta, was also executed, while thirteen slaves were sentenced to ten years in jail and another five to a hundred lashes.[314] Each of them was given lashes because they were suspected of being party to the plan and of having failed to report it. On whose testimony or evidence was this sentence passed? Was there another statement as well as that of Santiago, or were the sentences passed solely on the basis of his statement? These extremely perplexing questions still await satisfactory answers, because we have been unable to find the military court papers relating to this conspiracy. However, there is evidence that another slave, Francisco, owned by Juan M Almodóvar, had informed on other individuals of color from several plantations who were the ringleaders. They were fully abreast of the plans and were preparing to take part in the revolution. Nonetheless, Francisco was not given his freedom, unlike another informer, Santiago, who was additionally rewarded with three hundred pesos.[315]

CHAPTER
XI

"The Final Attempt":
The 1848 Slave Conspiracy
in Vega Baja

Long before the foundation of Vega Baja in 1776, the coastal lands of the district were being used to establish *hatos* and grow subsistence crops. The crops originally planted were potatoes, oranges, rice, corn, and, especially, bananas. It is a humid, flat region, ideal for any type of cultivation. The River Cibuco flows through these lands at the Cabo Caribe barrio, providing swift and easy transportation between the interior and the Atlantic coast.

At the beginning of the nineteenth century, a radical change took place in the history of Vega Baja agriculture. Once the *hatos* of the district had been broken up, subsistence farming was replaced by commercial agriculture based around sugar cane. Already by 1839, 54 per cent of all the cultivated land in Vega Baja was given over to sugar. This also happened, on a larger scale, in the Cabo Caribe barrio, to the north of the district of Vega Baja, where the original inhabitants—small landowners—immigrated to the area around Vega Alta in the interior of the island.

Between 1833 and 1839, as the plantations were being developed and many people from Vega Baja were emigrating, the number of slaves increased rapidly, from 282 to 426. In fact, more slaves were brought into Vega Baja in those six years than were imported over the fifty-five years preceding 1833.[316] Nevertheless, despite the increase in slaves, the main hacienda owners complained that they were not sufficient to satisfy the requirements of their plantations. For this reason much of the fertile land on their haciendas remained uncultivated.

The sugar plantations developed on a large scale between 1800 and 1830, occupying the most fertile land of the Cabo Caribe barrio. The majority of them were owned by Ramón Soler, Francisco Náter, Pedro Prado and Jacinto López. It was there that the largest numbers of slaves, the greatest number of *cuerdas* planted with cane and the best sugar technology were concentrated. The River Cibuco was also used to power the mills and for transporting the sugar manufactured at the haciendas to the port of Vega Baja.

Ramón Soler, a close friend of Governor de la Torre (1822-1836) and originally from Vizcaya in Spain, was an influential *elector pudiente* (1834) and city councillor in the capital (1848). He was also the owner of the Santa Inés, the largest hacienda in Vega Baja.[317] It produced over half of all the sugar from Vega Baja. In 1838, the Santa Inés produced 6,600 *quintales* of sugar valued at 16,500 pesos, 9,870 *cuartillos* of cane syrup valued at 2,364 pesos, and 4,200 *cuartillos* of rum valued at 2,520 pesos.[318] In that year the Santa Inés was cultivating cane on 200 of its 1,450 *cuerdas* and was running two iron sugarmills.[319] The hacienda also had two wooden houses and two barracoons for a workforce of 100 slaves. Of these, 78 were men and 22 women, 88 had been born in Africa, 11 in Puerto Rico, and 1 had been brought from Saint Croix.[320]

The hacienda of San Vicente, which belonged to Jacinto López, adjoined the Santa Inés. In 1838, it had 180 acres of cane producing 5,279 *quintals* of sugar valued at 13,175 pesos and 5,700 *cuartillos* of cane syrup valued at 1,366 pesos.[321] The workforce was composed of 33 slaves, 20 of whom were from Africa, 6 from Puerto Rico and 1 from Martinique.[322]

The other hacienda, which was smaller than the others, was the property of Francisco Náter. Here 30 acres of sugar were cultivated from which 1,200 *cuartillos* of cane syrup were extracted.[323] The workforce was made up of 19 slaves.[324]

Finally, the hacienda of Pedro Prado, an immigrant from Guatemala who was the alcalde of Vega Baja in 1838, cultivated 100 acres of cane producing 2,500 *quintales* of sugar valued at 6,250 pesos; 2,500 cuartillos of cane syrup valued at 600 pesos; and 1,300 *cuartillos* of rum valued at 780 pesos.[325] Sixty-eight slaves made up the workforce of his hacienda.[326]

In the year in question, 1838, the haciendas of Soler, López, Prado, and Náter monopolized sugar production in Vega Baja. Their production increased to comprise 99 per cent of all the sugar manufactured, 56 per cent of the cane syrup, and 24 per cent of the rum. They also owned 47 per cent of all the slaves in Vega Baja.

In the years that followed, the amount of land given over to growing cane on the haciendas of Soler, Prado, López, and Náter increased. Nevertheless, these hacendados continually complained of losses on their plantations. The available data for the value of the sugar produced by Soler and Prado on their haciendas reveal that this fell during the 1840s, and that, although the value rose during 1847, the year before the 1848 conspiracy, it was lower than in 1841. Between 1838 and 1848, the number of slaves on the haciendas of Soler, Prado, Náter, and López also rose. Soler increased his staff from 100 to 150 slaves and also employed 35 waged laborers in sugar manufacturing tasks.[327] Náter increased his staff from 30 to 41 slaves, J. López from 33 to 70 slaves, and Prado from 65 to 90 slaves.[328] However, despite the fact that they owned 365 of the 486 slaves in Vega Baja, they claimed not to have sufficient personnel to meet the requirements of their haciendas.[329]

As in the previous years, hacendados Soler, Náter, López, and Prado also continued to be prominent public officers in Vega Baja. Soler, for example, was a *regidor* of the capital (1842), an *elector pudiente* of Puerto Rico and an honorary *comisario de guerra* in the capital (1842); Prado was the town's alcalde in 1838 and *teniente de guerra* from 1838 to 1848, while Náter and López were *regidores* of the ayuntamiento of Vega Baja, in 1848 and 1841, respectively.

Despite their social, economic and political power in the 1840s, these hacendados found themselves embroiled in disputes with the neighboring merchant hacendados and the Vega Baja authorities. In 1840, Soler, Náter and other landowners refused to allow other residents to use the public jetty on the River Cibuco and, in March 1843, headed by Soler, they closed the highway leading to the port of Vega Baja, thus tripling the length of the journey to reach it.[330] In 1849, they were all accused of smuggling and breaking the law that required them to provide details of the quantity of products sent to the capital.[331] In 1841, Soler was also accused of not paying the *subsidio* to the ayuntamiento and of seeking to embarrass the ayuntamiento of Vega Baja.[332]

During these years, the slaves in Vega Baja and on the haciendas of Soler, Prado, Náter and López displayed their rejection of slavery in a number of ways. On May 5, 1831, Soler's "ill-treated" slaves set fire to his hacienda.[333] Severe measures had to be taken to prevent escapes. In 1832, some slaves tried unsuccessfully to escape to Santo Domingo in the boat 'San Pedro' which was anchored in the River Cibuco.[334] The slave conspiracies aroused so much concern among these hacendados that in 1837 the Ayuntamiento determined that the urban militiamen of Vega Baja should not go to Vega Alta to exercise as this force should be available for duty, owing to the increased number of slaves and the dense concentration of *bozales* in Vega Baja.[335] The Ayuntamiento also indicated that it should be equipped and ready for unforeseen circumstances. Four years later, on October 16, 1841, during a session of the Ayuntamiento, Soler, Náter, Prado and López, as hacendados of the neighbourhood, met with the town councillors to discuss the town's security. They concluded that they needed to build a stone house capable of containing the slave population.[336]

In the years preceding the conspiracy the slaves had lost confidence in the Síndico Defensor de Esclavos, Agustín Otero. A hacendado of Vega Baja and a slaveowner, Otero occupied this post from 1843 to 1848. In 1845, Joaquín, a slave of José M Rodríguez from the Ceyba quarter, complained to Otero of mistreatment by his foreman and excessive work at his hacienda.[337] Otero, rather than proceeding to investigate Joaquín's complaint, informed Diego Rodríguez, at that time manager of the hacienda, of what had happened. Rodríguez pointed out that Joaquín was a rogue and that was as far as the matter went. Meanwhile, Joaquín was placed in shackles for three months. As a result, since using legal channels had proved ineffectual, Joaquín and another ten slaves from Rodríguez' hacienda ran away on the night of July 11, 1845.[338]

The escape of slaves from Vega Baja, the fire at Soler's hacienda, the constant precautions to prevent possible slave uprisings, and the escape of slaves from Soler and Rodríguez' haciendas—all were examples of over fifteen years of struggle by slaves in Vega Baja. The process culminated in August 1848 with a slave conspiracy at the most important haciendas in Vega Baja.

From a financial point of view, the state of the Puerto Rican sugar industry at the start of 1848 was not very promising. The price per *quintal* had fallen to $5.14 on the island's main market in the United States. The high tariffs, the European wars, the lack of credit and other problems mentioned earlier kept the sugar plantations in crisis. This was exacerbated by the legal repression sanctioned by the Bando Negrero of General Prim which was issued in May 1848. This gave the masters the right to abuse their slaves, something that was unprecedented in the history of Puerto Rican slavery.[339] In August the slave conspiracy in Ponce was uncovered and it was there, two weeks later, that the slaves of Otero, Náter, López, Prado and Soler rose up.

The plans for the Vega Baja conspiracy are very similar to those of Ponce in July of the same year, already discussed in this book: attack the military garrison, seize the arms of the urban militia, and massacre the whites.[340] The conspiracy was denounced by one of those involved, Miguel "the mulatto," who informed his master, Francisco I. Náter, of the plans.[341]

The sources available do not allow us to develop a clear picture of the facts of the conspiracy. We do not know how or when the slaves met to carry it out. Nor do we know how many insurgents there were and whether all the slaves of Vega Baja and Cabo Caribe knew about the uprising and were intending to support it. In his statement, Miguel the mulatto pointed out that the conspirators had told him that they would escape to Santo Domingo if it failed.[342] It was in fact discovered that the conspiracy was to begin on a day when some boats were on the River Cibuco. These boats would be used in the case of defeat. Did the slaves believe they had little chance of success? What in fact was the real purpose of the conspiracy? To loot the haciendas, avenge themselves for abuses by the whites, and then flee?

Although we do not know whether the boats were on the River Cibuco, on the night of August 13, 1848, Florencio, an African aged 26 and a slave of the *síndico* Agustín Otero, ran away from his hacienda. He went quickly round the haciendas of Cabo Caribe uttering the password: "comrades, the time has come." Why, if the conspiracy was to start when the boats arrived on the River Cibuco, was Florencio, who lived in the Algarrobo quarter, chosen? How did Florencio find out about the uprising? How did he manage to escape without arousing suspicion? Perhaps the Algarrobo barrio did not have the same level of vigilance as Cabo Caribe? Perhaps Florencio was chosen because he was a slave of the Síndico and would therefore not be suspected? Cabo Carib, not Algarrobo, had been the scene of numerous clashes with the slaves, and the haciendas of Soler, Náter, López, and Prado, not that of Otero, had been the most affected. Furthermore, military surveillance was better in Cabo Caribe because the town and port of Vega Baja were located there.

We have no documentation recounting what happened when Florencio arrived at the Cabo Caribe haciendas and announced the start of the revolt. Possibly nothing of significance occurred as the conspiracy had been betrayed on the morning of the 13th. This had provided time for moving the local military regiments, as well as another fifty grenadiers from the Regimento de Granada, to Vega Baja.[343] However, the conspiracy apparently took its course as the slaves were unaware that Miguel had informed on them. The Regimento de Granada immediately crushed the conspiracy and Florencio was arrested. Apparently very few slaves took part since only fifty grenadiers were needed to suppress the uprising. Those who did revolt surrendered immediately.

After the insurgents had been arrested, an ordinary court martial held on August 23 sentenced "Black Miguel" to the death penalty. We do not have any evidence to explain why the most severe punishment was given to Miguel. Florencio, who had betrayed the conspiracy, was sentenced to eight years' imprisonment and "Big Manuel" to two years. Miguel, the mulatto informer, was rewarded with 100 pesos, 400 fewer than the 500 stipulated by the 1826 Reglamento de Esclavos. He was also not given his freedom, which was ordered by the Reglamento.

Agustín Otero, *the síndico procurador de esclavos* and the owner of Florencio, Jacinto, and Braulio, was fined 100 pesos for not keeping a close watch on his hacienda.[344]

Although 1848 was a critical year for the sugar plantations in Puerto Rico, the available documentation on the Vega Baja conspiracy does not give any indication as to whether this difficult situation obliged the hacendados to demand greater output from their slaves. We cannot exclude this as one of the reasons for the slave conspiracies. Unfortunately the bulk of the documentation is derived from news items that appeared in the *Gaceta Oficial de Puerto Rico* eleven days after the conspiracy was uncovered.[345] The article does not explain why this conspiracy was mentioned in the *Gaceta* and not other, more important ones. What was the government's intention in releasing a few—mostly confused—details? What we do know for certain is that this was the last slave conspiracy aimed at capturing the towns of Puerto Rico. From 1848 onwards slaves would continue to rise up but it would be in order to murder their *mayordomos* [overseers].

CHAPTER
XII

Homicides Perpetrated by Slaves, 1850–1873

On account of the numerous failed slave conspiracies in the first half of the nineteenth century, another type of collective protest against the institution of slavery became common from 1850 onwards: the murder of the *mayordomo* by a group of slaves. From 1840 onwards, we find various conspiracies, such as that in Naguabo in 1843 and in Toa Baja in 1846, the main objective of which was to murder the foreman. These two cases were the forerunners of what would subsequently become the most common form of protest against slavery on the eve of its abolition in Puerto Rico in 1873.

Naguabo, 1843

One of the first uprisings in which a *mayordomo* was murdered took place in the early morning of January 15, 1843, at Guillermo Bedlow's hacienda in Naguabo. An English immigrant from the British colony of Bermuda, Bedlow may have arrived on the island before 1822.[346] When he got there he purchased the La Fortuna hacienda in the Quebrada Las Palmas barrio. Although we do not know the exact date of his arrival in Puerto Rico it must have been shortly before the September 1822 slave conspiracy at several haciendas in the Quebrada Las Palmas barrio. On that occasion, Dubois, the leader of the Holstein conspiracy, attempted to recruit several slaves from those haciendas.[347] We have no evidence, however, to indicate that Bedlow's slaves were involved in this conspiracy, which was suppressed right from the start.

Bedlow bought the La Fortuna from Pedro Duclerc. It included slaves, 500 acres of land, an ox and a mill for crushing cane.[348] Between 1830 and 1843 the hacienda cultivated an average of fifty acres of cane and had a labor force composed of thirty slaves. Bananas and other minor crops were also grown. The hacienda was managed by Guillermo Noble. From the time Bedlow bought the hacienda up until the day of the conspiracy in 1843, he conducted several transactions of buying and selling slaves. He sold twelve and bought five. He also granted Manuel de Jesús, an African slave aged thirty whom Bedlow had bought from Duclerc when he purchased the hacienda, the right to buy his freedom for 300 pesos.[349] The process of *coartación* was completed when De Jesús managed to pay off his freedom in July 1842, sixteen months before the conspiracy. He settled his debt to Bedlow with a cow.[350]

As Bedlow did not inform the authorities that the debt had been paid and that De Jesús was now free he was obliged to stay at the hacienda for another sixteen months. It was only on January 12, 1843 that Bedlow formally notified the local authorities that De Jesús was a free man. Two days later, De Jesús headed a revolt along with his former slave companions.[351] At dawn on January 15 the slaves gathered at the hacienda of Brigadier Manuel Arroyo from where they all went to set fire to Bedlow's hacienda. Led by De Jesús, they attempted to take the manager of the hacienda, Guillermo Noble, by surprise and wounded him slightly. De Jesús also attacked Noble's wife, stabbing her several times. Meanwhile, the slaves set fire to two bagasse buildings at the La Fortuna hacienda, reducing them to ashes.

When the news reached the town, a military corps was marshalled to prevent the rebels from entering it. Troops from the district who were at the port were sent in. The alcalde, the commander, and a contingent of *matriculados* [seamen] also arrived at the hacienda. De Jesús ran away after they started to hunt him down in order to hang him. He was later found hanged.[352]

The military report does not give any information as to how and when the conspiracy was put into effect. Nor do we know the reason for the alliance between the slaves at Bedlow's hacienda and those from Arroyo's hacienda nor why the latter agreed to fight under De Jesús' leadership. Nor do we know where Bedlow was while all this was going on as apparently he not present. But even if he had been, it seems to us that Noble, the person who actually managed La Fortuna, was responsible to the slaves for what went on at the hacienda. This could explain why he and his wife were attacked. It could also explain why De Jesús, now a free man, wounded them. Was it because Noble was to blame for that fact that De Jesús had not been freed despite having purchased his freedom sixteen months previously?

Although the existing documentation mentions that two black slaves belonging to Brigadier Arroyo were arrested along with several of Bedlow's slaves, it does not state what punishments were meted out. However, in a letter to the Governor the Comandante de Marina did observe that this was an isolated incident and of no particular significance.[353]

Toa Baja, 1846

Another case where slaves rose up against the mayordomo, very similar to that in Baguabo in 1843, took place in Toa Baja during the cane harvest in March 1846. The murder was committed at the hacienda San Pedro, which belonged to Francisco Soler. He was the regidor of the Ayuntamiento of Toa Baja in 1846 as well as a prominent slave trader.[354] Between 1830 and 1840 he had been granted several licenses for bringing slaves onto the island. In 1824, he was granted a license to import 300 slaves.[355] These were not intended for his plantation but for sale. Soler paid four pesos in tax for each individual brought in.[356] On account of his many activities, Soler was frequently absent from his hacienda. Hence the running of the plantation was entrusted to the foreman Fernado Clotter, a free mulatto. It was precisely because he was a mulatto that the slaves and free laborers refused to obey him.

On the afternoon of April 28, 1846, the slaves and most of the free mulattoes rose up, refusing to take their food rations and go to work.[357] Clotter was killed by a free mulatto. The insurgents remained at the hacienda instead of running away or heading for the town of Toa Baja to attack it, as slaves from the same district had done successfully three years before.

Although the town was not in danger, the Captain General sent in a company of *cazadores de Iberia* under the command of a second corporal, along with other officers who set out from the capital. Hours later they disembarked at Palo Seco with the assistance of the Navy. Although they reached the hacienda almost a day later, everything was already quiet. The necessary punishment was carried out. It appears that Soler, to whom the slaves had presented their demands in person, had also arrived at this time.[358] They said that Clotter was wicked and strict but it was to no avail since the accused were immediately sent to jail and counteractive and security measures were put in place. As at Naguabo, the authorities downplayed the significance of the attempted rebellion, describing it as a riot.[359] The free mulatto who killed the foreman was hanged, which was what had also happened in Naguabo.[360]

Why did the slaves not run away from the hacienda since they knew what punishments awaited them? Why did they not attack the town? Why did they not plan a general conspiracy? In the absence of details, two hypotheses can be put forward to throw some light on these questions. The insurgent slaves knew of the executions and other severe punishments suffered by those who had taken part in the 1843 revolt. Following the many failures throughout the history of the struggle for freedom by their race in Toa Baja and the rest of Puerto Rico, they also knew that they had only one option: kill the foreman, take their revenge and then await their punishment.

Instant revenge by means of homicide, as illustrated by these two incidents from 1840-1850, was the most common form of protest against the institution of slavery in Puerto Rico in the ten years preceding its abolition 1873.

Over the following decades, murders of foremen proliferated throughout the island. Some of the incidents took place in the following locations:

Hacienda El Cacique (1853)
Hacienda Banardi, Mayagüez (1867)
Hacienda California, Maunabo (1867)
Hacienda Juan Buso, Naguabo (1868)
Hacienda Nicolás Márquez, Ponce (1869)

Hacienda Aguirre, Guayama (1870)
Hacienda La Monserrate, Dorado (1870)
Hacienda Castillo, Cabo Rojo (1870)
Hacienda Julita, la Capital (1870)

According to the records of the government of the island what was undoubtedly one of the most brutal murders occurred in 1867 in the Hacienda "La California" in Maunabo.[361] The disturbances commenced in the night of July 21, 1868, when Vicente, Primo, Gil, Juan Pablo, and José, young *bozal* slaves owned by Don Domingo Curer, ran away from the "La California" hacienda situated in the barrio of La Calzada.[362] The *bozales* crossed the island, from Maunabo in the southeast to Guaynabo in the north, where they were captured approximately ten days later.[363] On August 12, Don Francisco Molinary, the head *mayordomo*, went to look for them in Guaynabo and brought them back to "La California." They were immediately punished by the overseer with three lots of 25 lashes, in the presence of the second *mayordomo*, José María Colón, who had just been taken on at the hacienda, and Molinary himself. They were also placed in the stocks for the following eight days. Cared for and given treatment after the punishments, they returned to work under the watchful eye of Colón. According to Juan Pablo, over the month of labor that followed, Colón ill-treated them and obliged them to work faster. During that month, according to Molinary, the slaves' attitude was arrogant and bad-tempered.[364] As a result they were disciplined frequently and no two days went by without Colón punishing them with the whip.

At daybreak on September 3, 1868, Colón wakened the slave workforce of "La California," among whom were Vicente, Juan Pablo, Primo, José, and Gil. He ordered them to take a section of cane for cutting and weeding and, when they had finished that, to start on another.[365] Hoes were distributed for performing the task. The foreman went away until nine in the morning. When he returned to the sections where the *bozales* were, he noticed that while other slaves from the plantation had made progress, they were lagging behind.

Vicente was not working on account of pains in his chest. The slave Juan Pablo also asked to be sent to hospital. Then the foreman began to cry "TALA, TALA," and taking the stick he had and holding Juan Pablo by the hands, he attempted to hit him.[366] At that moment, Vicente landed a blow on his neck from behind with the hoe. This made Colón collapse. Juan Pablo sat on him and stabbed him in the throat; José held him by the feet and then they all attacked him, inflicting several wounds with the knives and machetes they had secretly brought with them.

Valentino, one of the slaves, heard the foreman's groans and went to the scene of the bloody homicide. He discovered the slaves with the murder weapons and told them they should not run away but go to the hacienda. Then he followed them, reporting to the foreman Juan Bruzano, who placed them in the stocks until he could send them to jail.

The military trial in the *alcaldía mayor* in Humacao extended over a period of two months. On November 8, 1867, Vicente and Juan Pablo were sentenced to death and Primo, José and Gil to eight years.[367] During the trial it was stressed that the ill treatment by Colón was not sufficient reason for killing him. It was also pointed out that the slaves had agreed on the murder beforehand.

In the light of this dangerous situation and perturbed by these events—in particular that in Maunabo—the civil governor, José Laureano Sanz, in a highly confidential letter dated May 4, 1870, ordered the local administration to conduct a covert investigation in tandem with the alcaldes and *corregidores* in the districts that had large numbers of slaves.[368] He asked that, in order to avoid serious problems for the government, they should observe the Reglamento de Esclavos of August 1826.

When indicating the possible causes of the homicides, Governor Sanz explained that there were two main ones. First, the masters' greed, since, realizing that slavery would be abolished in a few years' time, they were attempting to extract maximum usage from their slaves. That was the reason for the intensified and increased workload and the severe discipline that went beyond reasonable limits. Another factor was the abolitionist, separatist, and reformist propaganda that had incited the slaves to seek revenge.

In response to the governor's order, between July and September 1870 the *alcaldías mayores* in Puerto Rico submitted their observations. These were all very different and revealed concern not only about the slave population but also about the situation of the free laborers.[369]

Conclusion:
Slave Conspiracies and Uprisings
in Puerto Rico, 1796–1848

In the period between 1795 and 1848 slaves in Puerto Rico collective-ly manifested their repudiation of the slavery system in two ways: by directly confronting the system and by running away. The former was the most common method—openly opposing the laws, institutions, landowners, mayordomos, and, in many cases, anyone who stood in the way of the insurgents' objectives.

Although the main focus of this book is the collective movements that directly confronted the slavery system, it is important to point out that between 1795 and 1848 there were also instances of slave escapes in Puerto Rico. Athough these were not active and direct protests against the institution of slavery, they also represented a form of rejection.

Individual escapes were more common than conspiracies. The notices of runaway slaves which appeared in the *Gaceta Oficical de Puerto Rico* between 1820 and 1865 have allowed us to reach a num-ber of conclusions. The escapes were mostly carried out by lone slaves.[370] Although there are several exceptions and in one case 34 managed to escape, as happened in Toa Baja in 1827 and in Vega Baja in 1845, it is clear that most escapes were individual rather than col-lective. Also, the majority of those who ran away were *bozales* and predominantly male. The ages of the fugitives ranged between 21 and 30. The older the slave, the less likely was he to run away.

The likelihood of success for the majority of escapes, by individu-als, was very slight. One, two or three runaways acting alone were incapable of defeating a squad of urban militiamen, or of outwitting the brutal men and the bulldogs that were undoubtedly searching for them from the moment of their escape. This could explain why there were apparently no maroon settlements on the island.

Another reason is that individual escapes did not lead to the rapid formation of large groups of maroons or runaway slaves. These maroon communities needed to be formed immediately after the escape. They were essential for subsequently assembling a fighting force and for developing maroon settlements with the defense capability to fight against the regular armies and preserve their hiding places for a reasonably long period of time.

The other explanation for the absence of maroon settlements on the island is the effectiveness of the press as a means of spreading news of runaways. As soon as a slave had escaped the *Gaceta Oficial de Puerto Rico* would publish a detailed description of the fugitive or fugitives. The item with the description ran for several months and almost always proved effective. As is clearly demonstrated by the news reports in the *Gaceta*, most of these slaves were captured.

Finally, the geography of Puerto Rico is the fourth reason why there were no maroon communities. The island's territorial limitations and the lack of expanses of uncultivated land, forests, mountainous areas, deserts or high precipices meant there were no natural refuges or shelters for runaway slaves. Nor did it facilitate guerilla warfare, the only defense option for the maroon communities. A conventional confrontation with the island's military forces would have been disastrous for the fugitives. In Puerto Rico there are no wildernesses, like those which harbored the maroon communities such as Palmares in northeastern Brazil in what is today the state of Pernambuco, nor mountainous areas as in Jamaica or the Cuban Sierra Maestra.

Collective escapes, on the other hand, took a different form from individual ones. This was especially so because Haiti, now a free nation ruled by former slaves, offered an extremely secure political refuge and a safe haven for Puerto Rican maroons. During the period under study (1795-1873), the military reports produced following the collective escapes in Puerto Rico constantly reiterate the allegation that the fugitives were planning to escape or had already escaped to Santo Domingo, under Haitian domination between 1822 and 1841—or to Haiti itself. We do not know whether the runaways from Puerto Rico reached their destination or what eventually became of them. Nevertheless, one can be sure that the slaves had hopes that they would be free once they reached Haiti. Even during the last slave

conspiracy in 1848 in the town of Vega Baja, the informer stated—
44 years after slavery had been abolished in Haiti—that the slaves
planned to begin the struggle as soon as some boats had dropped
anchor in the River Cibuco. These would take the slaves to Haiti if
the revolt was unsuccessful.

The Haitian Revolution (1794-1804) provided an example of struggle for slaves in Puerto Rico. In 1795, the authorities reported that the
conspiracy in the district of Agudailla had been inspired by that revolution.[371] Sixteen years later, in 1812, the slave Antonio from the district of Rio Piedras publicly urged others to take part in a rebellion.
He stated defiantly that, if they were not given their freedom, as
promised by the English, more blood would flow in Puerto Rico than
had been shed in Guarico in Haiti.[372]

As we have shown, there is no doubt that the Haitian experience
had a great influence on slaves in Puerto Rico but we believe that
many of the references made by Spanish officers were exaggerations
prompted by fear and, in many cases, based on inaccurate information. On the other hand, this justified the repression of the slaves and
the blacks. For example, in spite of the fact that the authorities were
able to describe the Haitian emissary Chaulette, even pointing out
that he was a polyglot, he was never captured nor was he ever heard
of again.[373] Nevertheless, serious precautionary measures were implemented that resulted, among other things, in a decree issued to the
local Ayuntamientos. They were to draw up lists of the black population and report on their activities and where they gathered. Another
example was Holstein's failed conspiracy of 1822. On that occasion
Governor Miguel de la Torre accused President Boyer of Haiti of
involvement in the conspiracy.[374] The accusations later turned out to
be false. As a rule, whenever there was a manifestation against slavery, the authorities claimed that Haiti was directly implicated, either
with the promise of arms and munitions or direct assistance from
their armies.

During the period from 1795 to 1848—the historical background
for this book and a period of unprecedented development for the
sugar industry and the parallel but disproportionate growth of the

Puerto Rican slave population—there were over twenty instances of slave conspiracies, revolts, or uprisings on the island (see Table X). The first revolt that we know of occurred in 1795 on a hacienda in Aguadilla, apparently as a direct result of the large amount of liberatory propaganda emanating from Haiti. Sixteen years later, in 1812, a large-scale conspiracy and the beginning of an uprising erupted on the outskirts of the capital. This spread from the town of El Roble in Río Piedras in the northeast as far as Añasco in the northwest.

TABLE X
Summary: Slave Conspiracies and Uprisings in Puerto Rico (1795–1848)

District	Date of incident	Official designation	Carried out	Betrayed	Military intervention
Aguadilla	October 3, 1795	Revolt	Yes	No	?
Humacao	1805	Captured the Casa del Rey	Yes	No	?
Capital	January 8, 1812	Revolt	Yes	Yes	Regimientos voluntarios de la patria urbanos
Bayamón	July 1821	Conspiracy	No	Yes	Regimiento de Granada
Barranquitas	June 11, 1821	Disorder	Yes	No	?
Guayama	July 27, 1822	Conspiracy	No	Yes	Regimiento de Granada
Naguabo	July 27, 1822	Conspiracy	No	Yes	Regimiento de Granada
Ponce	July 18, 1826	Conspiracy	No	Yes	Regimiento de Granada

TABLE X (Continued)
Summary: Slave Conspiracies and Uprisings in Puerto Rico (1795–1848)

District	Date of incident	Official designation	Carried out	Betrayed	Military intervention
Guayama	December 16, 1828	Attempted uprising	Yes	No	Urbanos
Vega Baja	May 5, 1831	Uprising	Yes	No	Urbanos
Ponce	January 20, 1833	Uprising	Yes	No	Urbanos
Ponce	January 17, 1835	March	Yes	No	Urbanos
Vega Baja	1838		No	No	Urbanos
Ponce	August 16, 1839	Disturbances	Yes	No	Urbanos
Guayanilla	September 26, 1840	Conspiracy	No	No	Urbanos
Ponce	December 19, 1841	Conspiracy	No	Yes	Regimiento de Granada
Isabela	January 1, 1841	Revolt	Yes	No	Urbanos
Naguabo	January 15, 1843	Uprising	Yes	No	Urbanos
Toa Baja	March 26, 1843	Uprising	Yes	No	Urbanos
Toa Baja	April 28, 1846	Uprising	Yes	No	Milicia disciplinada
Ponce	July 19, 1842	Conspiracy	No	Yes	Urbanos
Vega Baja	August 20, 1848	Uprising	Yes	Yes	Regimiento de Granada

In 1821 approximately 1,500 slaves—mainly from Bayamón, Toa Baja, Toa Alta, Guaynabo and Río Piedras—plotted unsuccessfully against the slavery system. Throughout the following year, slaves in Guaynabo and Naguabo were involved in a conspiracy which the authorities linked to the one organized by Docoudray Holstein. Many of the rebellious slaves who took part in these movements were *bozales*, that is, recently brought from Africa. They had a greater measure of rebelliousness in their blood than the naturalized or assimilated slaves. We know that the earliest slave revolts took place on board the slave ships. The 1826 conspiracy in Ponce followed the classic pattern of direct confrontation with the authorities by slaves who had recently arrived on the island. The conspirators had come to Puerto Rico only a few months earlier. A strong feeling of social solidarity developed among the *bozales*.

Following this conspiracy Governor Miguel de la Torre became aware that a serious problem was developing which threatened the peace of loyal subjects. As a result the Reglamento de Esclavos was issued in 1826. The Reglamento was pre-emptive and in this respect very different to the previous Slave Code of 1789 which, according to its introduction, aimed to protect slaves from being badly treated by their masters. The 1826 Reglamento, on the other hand, attempted to protect the masters from abuse by the slaves. There are two key factors that account for the differences between the two codes. In the first place, the growth of the slave population: in 1794 there were 17,500 slaves whereas by 1827 there were 31,874, more densely concentrated on the plantations of Puerto Rico. Secondly, there was now a revolutionary experience that had created a republic of former slaves. This was a lesson that slaves in Puerto Rico had already begun to learn, whether in the capital in 1812, in Bayamón in 1821, in Guayama and Naguabo in 1822, or in Ponce in 1826.

Between 1826 and 1840—years that marked the incorporation of the Puerto Rican sugar industry onto the international market as a large-scale producer—there was a period of economic and political stability. As a result, the importance of movements that confronted the slavery system declined. However, there were a number of small uprisings, in which slaves from one or two plantations participated. These minor uprisings and conspiracies took place at haciendas in Guayama in 1828, in Vega Baja in 1832, in Ponce in 1833 and in Guayanilla in 1840.

At the end of the 1830s the sugar industry began to experience a series of problems, the reasons for which were located on and off the island. This caused the seeds of slave rebellion to sprout once more, as had happened in the 1820s, one of the most significant being the large-scale conspiracy in Ponce in December 1841, which was coordinated with other districts. There were also three revolts, triggered by different reasons, such as those against mulatto foremen in Naguabo and Toa Baja and an uprising in Isabela to demand the observance of the 1826 Reglamento. In 1848 the two final collective conspiracies were carried out: one in Ponce and the other in the Cabo Caribe barrio of Vega Baja.

The uprisings were concentrated on the north coast, mainly in the area between Bayamón and Vega Baja, and on the south coast, mainly around Ponce, where there were five collective manifestations against the slavery system.

Most of the large sugar plantations in Puerto Rico were concentrated in the coastal areas of the island, and thus it was there that the highest proportion of slaves was to be found. The vast majority of those who joined these twenty insurgent movements came from these sugar plantations. It was enslaved labor in the canefields that by 1829 enabled Puerto Rico to manufacture sugar in sufficient quantities to compete on the international market. By 1840 the island was the world's tenth largest producer. It was also these laborers who were the main protagonists of most of the uprisings.

The rural slaves reacted in a very different manner from the urban slaves. The latter rarely took part in collective movements and when they did, it was in collaboration with slaves who worked in the canefields. The rural slaves, unlike their urban domestic counterparts, were continually at the mercy of price fluctuations on the international market as well as the lack of buyers for the sugar, the high customs tariffs and the effects of natural disasters such as drought or cholera. There were a few exceptions such as the 1812 conspiracy in the capital city in which domestic slaves played an active role. But even in this case, as in all the others, it was in association with and under the leadership of rural slaves.

In Puerto Rico slaves did not have real legal channels for effecting changes in their status. They were objects to be bought and sold and they did not have a legal personality. Their relationship with the law had to be conducted indirectly, through a *síndico procurador de esclavos*. But there is no evidence in the instances of collective movements of any reformist or humanist intervention on the part of these legal intermediaries. In fact, the *síndicos procuradores* in the districts where revolts occurred were slaveowners, hacendados and prominent political figures. They could not avoid being directly affected by the revolts since their slaves also participated in these insurrectionist movements. Such is the case, for example, of the *síndico procurador* Agustín Otero from the town of Vega Baja, who was the owner of the leaders of the 1848 revolt in that district.

Another aspect of our study of slaves in terms of the legal system is as follows: slaves in Puerto Rico were aware that other European nations had abolished slavery in their Caribbean colonies by legal methods and that Spain was the only power that had not done likewise. Meanwhile, the *gobierno superior* of Puerto Rico insisted that violence was not the means to achieve freedom, but nonetheless rejected the idea of reforming the institution and much less of abolishing it. Throughout the first half of the nineteenth century, instead of reform, it intensified the repressive and pre-emptive measures. In fact, the core of the 1826 Reglamento de Esclavos, like other subsequent slave legislation, was aimed at suppressing conspiracies, not introducing reforms. When a situation that was not anticipated by the Reglamento arose, legislation was immediately drawn up to deal with it. In 1834, it was forbidden to bring Methodist bibles onto the island because they were subversive and corrupted the minds of slaves since they advocated the absolute equality of whites, mulattoes and black slaves.[375] Therefore, as no real legal channels were open to them, for most slaves violence was the only means of obtaining their freedom.

Aim of the conspiracies

A pressing desire for freedom was the main reason behind most of the collective uprisings. However, there were several that were not aimed at obtaining freedom. A good example being the 1838 uprising in the Barrio Corto de los Laureles in Ponce, when the slaves refused to work on another master's plantation, and the 1846 uprising in Toa Baja, the aim of which was to murder the *mayordomo*. Another exception was the one in 1841 in Isabela. On that occasion, thirty-six

slaves—men, women, and children—left the hacienda of Tomás Pamias. Carrying their farming tools and the food distributed on that day, they walked to the town to demand the implementation of the second chapter of the 1826 Reglamento de Esclavos, which prohibited anyone from compelling their slaves to work on a Sunday. This was a unique case, because the slaves used violent means to demand the implementation of the very code that legally subjected them to enslavement.

It was only in two of the conspiracies that the movement to liberate the slaves was linked to the struggle for political independence in Puerto Rico. The first occurred simultaneously in Naguabo and Guayama and was organized alongside the 1822 conspiracy of Docoudray Holstein. The slave uprisings were planned to coincide with a military expedition made up of mercenaries, European and Latin American, West Point cadets, adventurers, ex-soldiers from the Spanish American wars of independence, Philadelphia merchants and journalists from the United States. The conspiracy planned to create the "República Boricua" with the help of the slaves, who were the most vulnerable sector in terms of the revolutionary transformation of Puerto Rico. Who better to support the political aims of the whites!

Holstein's insurgents believed that slavery would be abolished after the battle and that the freed slaves would devote themselves to fighting for the liberation of Puerto Rico. However, the leaders of this expedition never really intended to abolish slavery definitively. They planned to make use of the enslaved force during the war but when the republic was established they would be enslaved once again. Holstein justified his plans by the fact that, like the hacendados and the Spanish bureaucracy in Puerto Rico, he believed that enslaved labor was the only way to keep agriculture, and therefore sugarcane, profitable.

Another expedition that intended to fight for the independence of Puerto Rico as well as free the slaves was that of General Mariño from Santo Domingo. Although the documentation is unclear about this alleged invasion, it was apparently important because the authorities discovered that, if Mariño's venture succeeded, he would divide up the island of Puerto Rico so as to turn every former slave into a small landowner.

After the failure of the conspiracies of Holstein and Mariño as well as that of 1837, we have no evidence of any other events linking the Puerto Rico independence movement to the slave conspiracies. However, towards the end of the 1860s, when the most important separatist rebellion on the island broke out, the military authorities reported important findings linking the separatists' revolutionary plans to the slaves. Colonel Gamal, of the General Staff in Arecibo, reported that in 1866, almost a year before the revolt in Lares, abolitionists were inciting the slaves. Gamal suspected that if a separatist attempt was carried out this would begin in places close to districts with large numbers of slaves.[376] Two years later, on September 29, 1868, an independence conspiracy was being planned in Lares. This date was specifically chosen because the slaves had their day off.[377] It is clear that the separatists were confident of the slaves' participation. But the conspiracy was uncovered and, as is known, they were forced to bring it forward six days to September 23. Several separatist leaders took their slaves to Lares, offering them their freedom in return for taking part in the uprising. These were Bernal, Angleró, Laracuente, Muz and in particular the brothers Beauchamp, the wealthy owners of coffee plantations in the Furnias barrio of Mayagüez. The Beauchamps took their slaves to Lares and en route the latter looted the shops owned by Spaniards. This was one of the most violent episodes of the Lares uprising.[378] Other slaves ran away spontaneously and took part on the night of the revolt. Meanwhile, the provisional government in Lares ordered that any slave who took up arms would be freed as would "all those who had been prevented from doing so."[379]

In the adjoining districts of Añasco and Peñuelas the militia companies were ordered to be placed under arms because the El Pepino insurrection could have been linked to the slaves.[380] In San Germán, following the escapes, other methods were taken to punish the slaves.[381] In places as far away as the Pellot hacienda in the district of Guayama, it was reported that the slaves were awaiting their freedom and would immediately rise up in arms if they were not granted it.[382]

The prospects were very bleak, both for separatists and slaves, when hours later, during the military campaign in the district of El Pepino at San Sebastián, the insurrection was crushed and completely destroyed.

During the trial of those accused of taking part in the Lares uprising, 46 slaves were questioned on suspicion of being conspirators.[383] As Table XI illustrates, they came mainly from Mayagüez (15), San Sebastián (10), and San Germán (10).

TABLE XI
Slaves Prosecuted Following the Lares Uprising

Name of slave	Owner	Town
1. Simón	Ambrosio Angleró	Mayagüez
2. Bautista	Ambrosio Angleró	Mayagüez
3. Juan Santos	Miguel Font	Pepino
4. Miguel	Ambrosio Angleró	Mayagüez
5. José	Víctor Serrano	Pepino
6. Balbino	Víctor Serrano	Pepino
7. Narciso	Víctor Serrano	Pepino
8. Evaristo	Víctor Serrano	Pepino
9. Pablo	Víctor Serrano	Pepino
10. Juan	Luis Colen	San Juan

TABLE XI (Continued)
Slaves Prosecuted Following the Lares Uprising

Name of slave	Owner	Town
11. Lorenzo Valentín	Not listed	Mayagüez
12. Toribio	Not listed	Guayanilla
13. Valentín	Eugenio Bernal	Mayagüez
14. Juan	Eugenio Bernal	Mayagüez
15. Bernardo	Not listed	Mayagüez
16. Francisco	Not listed	Mayagüez
17. Girau	Manuel Mangual	Añasco
18. Timoteo	Not listed	Mayagüez (African-born)
19. Pancacio	Pablo Beauchamp	Mayagüez
20. Manuel	Laracuente	Caguas
21. José	Laracuente	Caguas
22. Luis	Not listed	Mayagüez
23. Cándido	Pedro Beauchamp	Mayagüez
24. Solinario	Not listed	San Germán
25. Juan Pío	Juan Dolen	San Germán
26. Juan	Domingo Chiveconfi	San Germán
27. Alejandro	Juan Cavirres	Aguadilla
28. Sifredo	Tomás Soro	Pepino
29. Juan Pedro	Not listed	Mayagüez
30. Miguel	Not listed	San Germán
31. Alejandro	Ibolione	San Germán
32. Bartolomé	Ibolione	San Germán
33. Avelina	Ibolione	San Germán
34. Antonio	Ibolione	San Germán
35. Manuel Daniel	Ibolione	San Germán
36. Antonio	Eugenio Bernal	Mayagüez
37. Guillermo	Aniceto Pérez	Isabela
38. Tiburcio	Juan Juarbe	Isabela
39. Juan Pablo Cardona	Freedman	Aguadilla
40. Victorio	Not listed	Mayagüez
41. Anacleto	Not listed	San Germán
42. Lino	Colón	Lares

TABLE XI (Continued)
Slaves Prosecuted Following the Lares Uprising

Name of slave	Owner	Town
43. Trinidad	Plumey	Lares
44. José	Miguel Font	Pepino
45. Juan de la Cruz	Miguel Font	Pepino
46. Lioricio	Alejandro Alers	Pepino

Conditions under which the conspiracies took place

Let us examine the circumstances that gave rise to the conspiracies. The reasons which motivated the slaves to take part in these twenty acts of rebellion vary according to the conditions that governed their lives. Although it is scientifically impossible to develop an explanatory theoretical model for all the conspiracies, it is clear that some of the reasons why the slaves were motivated to rebel reappeared again and again. Let us look more closely at three factors that we believe can help to account for several conspiracies and uprisings between 1795 and 1848.

1. The high percentage of *bozales* brought from Africa between 1820 and 1830 is one of the most important factors behind the revolts, escapes and murders of mayordomos in Puerto Rico carried out by the enslaved population. The African-born *bozales*, more than the other slaves, resisted the work regime to which they were subjected when they arrived on the island. Those who rebelled in Bayamón in 1822 and in Ponce in 1826 had arrived only a few months before the conspiracy. The ones who fought most resolutely against their owners for over half a century were the "negros cabezones" [pigheaded blacks]. They were the leaders of the Ponce conspiracy of 1841 and slaves from the Longoba nation in Toa Baja in 1843, as well as those in Vega Baja in 1840.

2. Despite the fact that the slaves had some knowledge of the events in Haiti, Spain, Puerto Rico and other places where slavery

was under discussion, their heartfelt desire for freedom gave rise to striking errors of interpretation. This was the case of the 1812 conspiracy in the capital, during which the slaves insisted that slavery had been abolished but that the Spanish officers were disregarding this royal decree.

3. The recurring economic recessions in Puerto Rico and their repercussions on the situation of slaves who worked in the canefields is another reason for their collective defiance. Fluctuations in the price of sugar, droughts, high export tariffs, technological backwardness, the lack of ships, the shortage of slaves and other problems on the international market were some of the reasons for these recessions. In the 1840s, for example, prices fell considerably, reaching the lowest amount ever paid. To avoid greater losses, some sugarmen increased the number of *cuerda*s cultivated with cane. Each slave was obliged to work more *cuerda*s. On many plantations during these periods, the privileges granted to them were removed so as to oblige the slaves to work full time on the plantation. One privilege was the use of small plots on the master's hacienda for growing crops and subsistence. During these years the slaves experienced hunger and, as the alcalde of Guayama aptly and vividly observed "let us remember that the man who is hungry is terrible."[384]

Plans

Let us now examine the plans for the conspiracies. The fact that a large number of them were planned in advance and called for sophisticated, large-scale and careful implementation, indicates the huge importance the slaves placed on organizing, preparing and awaiting the right conditions for carrying out a revolution which had some chance of success.

These subversive movements were characterized by their careful preparation. The insurgents attempted to obtain detailed knowledge about the strength of the opposition, the places where the district's weapons were hidden, that is the military garrison, and finally, the layout of the region. The 1841 slave conspiracy in Ponce reveals how the slaves operated; they waited four months to carry it out. During those four months word spread throughout the haciendas of Ponce and Juana Díaz. One factor that facilitated this was the freedom of movement enjoyed by slaves who worked away from the canefields such as, for example, oxen drivers. In the Ponce conspiracy the slaves planned to divide the insurgent armies into four groups. One would set fire to the hacienda of Doña Inés Guillermety which adjoined the town. Another group would hide on the road leading into town from the burning hacienda to attack the inhabitants of the neighboring estates who arrived to put out the fire. The third group of slaves was to hide in the countryside at the exit of the town to attack those coming from other areas to do the same. Other slaves would be in the town square celebrating the New Year and performing the bomba dance. This fourth group would take possession of the Casa del Rey, the place where the weapons were stored that would be used by the urban militiamen to quash the rebellion. They also built two small forts on the road out of town going towards the port of Ponce.

It was at the stage when the large-scale plans were being disseminated among the enslaved population that this conspiracy, like seven other similar collective movements, was betrayed. Over half of these collective movements were suppressed before the slaves had the chance to begin planning the struggle. The slaves with whom they shared the plans so that they would take part in the conspiracy were the ones who betrayed it. There were enormous but unavoidable risks at the diffusion stage. One reason for the high incidence of traitors was the fact that any slave reporting a conspiracy was rewarded with their freedom and five hundred pesos, as stipulated by the 1826 Code. However, this recommendation was rarely complied with.

The case of a slave called Marcos, the property of Mr. FM Tristany, who betrayed the famous 1841 slave revolt of Ponce, is one of the most interesting. He claimed that he was betraying the uprising because he did not bear any grudges against the white population and because his master, Mr. Tristany, whom he loved very much, was his godfather.

The conspiracies in which only a few slaves participated, and which were more spontaneous and were put into operation immediately, proved to be more effective. There was no time for them to be betrayed and they could be put into action. This was the case in the district of Toa Baja in 1843, when a group of slaves of the Longoba nation rose up following an afternoon of a game of *bolas*, and attacked and seized the Casa del Rey in the town.[385]

Similar strategies were planned and employed in most of these conspiracies. Three of the most important subversive tactics were probably the following:

1. Using authorized activities as a means of disguising or camouflaging a conspiracy, for example, Sunday mass and the bomba dances on the feastdays of Catholic saints such as San Miguel. This is illustrated by the Bayamón conspiracy of 1821 and the 1826 Ponce uprising. The bomba dance was one of the most common outlets for feelings of suppressed rage and rebelliousness as well as for planning conspiracies. This is why the authorities insisted that dances could not be held without government permission.[386]

2. Setting fire to the canefields and waiting nearby to attack those who came to put out the flames.

3. Promptly capturing the "Casa del Rey," where the weapons and munitions were stored that would be used by the urban militias to crush any conspiracy. In only one instance did the slaves manage to seize the arms. This was during the Toa Baja rebellion of 1843.

The military reaction was important. When these movements were developing it was shown that the urban militias, made up of citizens from each district, were inadequate in times of slave conspiracy or rebellion. For this reason, the local authorities had to seek military assistance from the Regimentos de Granada. The regiments were the official armies of the Spaniards in Puerto Rico and were composed of hired Spanish soldiers who were badly paid, had limited equipment and could not be mobilized rapidly. This inadequate military security explains the repressive measures taken against the enslaved population. It also shows the state of constant fear in which the hacendados and officers in Puerto Rico lived.

Any news of a revolt or conspiracy discovered in the Antilles was sufficient to generate immediate pre-emptive measures, mainly in the regions which had large concentrations of slaves. During the racial wars in Guadeloupe and Martinique and in Saint Croix in 1848, General Prim, the military governor of Puerto Rico, not only informed and alerted all the districts on the island to the threat, but also sent five hundred men to help suppress the revolutionaries in Saint Croix. It was during this period that Prim drew up the Código Negrero, in which the free blacks, mulattoes and descendants of Africans were considered to belong in the same category as the slaves.[387]

Punishments

One of the harshest forms of repression was the death penalty for slaves who took part in a conspiracy. This was applied as a punishment but it also acted as a deterrent for the survivors. The death penalty was imposed on five occasions, all of them at a time when the frequency and the importance of the slaves' collective movements had grown. On the other hand, during periods of economic growth and political stability, as in the 1830s, those accused were not sentenced to death but were put in jail, given lashes, expelled from Puerto Rico, or forced to labor in public works.

This situation changed radically during the 1840s when the sugar industry entered a period of crisis. The slaves began to conspire and the government reacted forcefully, not only by applying the death penalty to suspected conspirators but also by issuing the Slave Code of 1848. This code justified any aggression on the part of whites towards Africans or their descendants.

This type of collective rebellion by slaves in Puerto Rico was reaching a climax during the 1840s. After the enslaved population was decimated by cholera in 1855, and all uprising attempts to capture towns or haciendas had failed, the most rebellious opted for other forms of insurrection, the most common being the furtive and premeditated homicide of the *mayordomos* of haciendas. Some of these murders occurred in Aguadilla (1867), Naguabo (1868), Dorado (1869), Ponce

(1869), and especially the district of Maunabo in 1867, where five *bozales* brutally murdered their *mayordomo*.[388] The incident at "La California" was typical of the episodes that characterize the history of slave homicides in Puerto Rico. Finally, on account of their crimes during this period, slaves were the group most often condemned to the scaffold in the years preceding the abolition of slavery in 1873.[389]

Notes

Notes to Chapter I

1. Salvador Perea, *Historia de Puerto Rico (1537-1700)*. Instituto de Cultura Puertorriqueña and Universidad Católica de Puerto Rico (1972), p. 19.

2. Eugenio Fernández Méndez, *Historia Cultural de Puerto Rico*, Editorial Universitaria (1975), p. 127.

3. Although the history of Puerto Rican sugar is rather obscure (especially for the first centuries), and despite the fact that there is very little that can be stated definitively, it is worth pointing out some of the reasons for this slow growth. First, Spain's lack of interest in settling Puerto Rico and its focus on the kingdoms of Nueva España and Nueva Granada. Added to this was the exodus to South America of the island's early colonists, propelled by an insatiable desire for gold and silver. Second, the island's lack of capital, essential for establishing the sugarmills. Third, the decline of mining. The island lacked not only gold and silver, but also other metals such as copper which could, for example, have been used to build the *trapiches* and other equipment that was essential for establishing sugar plantations and sugar mills. Fourth, the handicap of the Spanish commercial monopoly, which made it impossible to expand the market for the island's sugar. For example, in 1746, exporting rum from Puerto Rico was prohibited because it competed with Spanish alcohol production. Fifth, sugar exports from Puerto Rico to the Spanish market were always limited by the fact that other sugar colonies dominated the peninsular market. In the sixteenth century, Granada and Hispaniola supplied sugar to the metropole. At the end of this century, between 1580 and 1640, they were replaced by Brazil. In the eighteenth century, Cuba became the main supplier of sugar to Spain. Sixth, the virtual lack of ships for transporting the island's sugar production to foreign markets. In 1660, Governor Juan Pérez de Guzmán complained that no registered ships had arrived in over eleven years, and as a result the inhabitants were left with no outlets for their products.

4. Gerard, Pierre Charles. *La economía haitiana en vías de desarrollo.* Mexico, Cuadernos Americanos, 1965.

5. For Guadeloupe and Saint Lucia, see John E. Baur, *International*

Repercussions of the Haitian Revolution. "The Americas" (April 1970), p. 405. For Cuba, see Philip Foner, *Historia de Cuba y sus relaciones con Estados Unidos,* p.67. For Venezuela, see JJ Oscariz, *La Rebelión de Esclavos en Bucamgua.* "Anuario de Escritos Americanos" (Seville) 28, L19707, p. 558-59.

6. Archivo General de las Indias – Ultramar, Legajo 6375. Carta reservada Núm. 2. Ramón de Castro a su Majestad, 22 January 1795. This incident is described as an insurrection.

7. *Ibid.*

8. *Ibid.* The documentation available for this insurrection is very sparse. Although Governor de Castro himself, as already mentioned, stressed the influence of French propaganda, we do not know in what form news of the abolition of slavery in Haiti (1794) spread among the island's slave population. Nor can we indicate whether there were other more immediate causes to explain why insurrection only occurred in Aguadilla and not other parts of the island. On the other hand, one must bear in mind that there were perhaps other uprisings and that we do not know about them because of the lack of municipal documents for this period.

9. AGPR. Fondo Documental: Manatí, Legajo 1812, Circular No. 37 Gobernador Toribio Montes, 3 November 1805.

10. AMM. Toribio Montes. Registro Núm. 1812, Núm. 37, Legajo Núm. 63. 3 November 1805.

11. *Ibid.*

12. AMM. Toribio Montes. Número 44. 23 January 1806.

13. *Ibid.*

14. *El proceso abolicionista en Puerto Rico,* Doc. Núm. 38, 13 November 1807 (MIC in CIH).

15. *Ibid.*

16. AGPR. Fondo Documental de los Gobernadores, Seguridad Pública, 10 January 1810, caja 175.

17. AGPR. Fondo Documental de los Gobernadores. Angel Laborde al Excelentísimo Capitán General de Puerto Rico. 17 November 1822. In this letter Laborde denies a possible relationship between Boyer and Holstein.

18. AGPR. Fondo Documental de los Gobernadores, Seguridad Pública, 25 April 1825, caja 186. The document describes Tristany as a light-skinned mulatto from the Santo Domingo council.

Notes to Chapter II

19. Philip S. Foner. *Historia de Cuba y sus relaciones con Estados Unidos.* Vol. 1, Instituto Cubano del Libro, Havana, 1973. Editorial de Ciencias Sociales, p. 96.

20. *Ibid.*

21. AHN. Documentos Españoles. A. XLVIII, 8-d, Microfilm in CIH. Francisco de Salazar. *Proceso abolicionista en Puerto Rico: Documentos para su estudio.* Vol. I, p. 125, Circular 75.

22. *Ibid.*

23. *Ibid.*, p.125.

24. *Ibid.*, p. 124.

25. In Cangrejos the racial imbalance was even more marked than in Río Piedras. The population consisted of 460 free blacks, 127 free mulattoes, 99 slaves and only 123 whites. A racial imbalance of this proportion would not have gone unnoticed by the authorities. From the earliest times when blacks were brought to the Americas, the Spanish authorities were always aware of this problem, since it was the primary condition for facilitating the start of a slave uprising; the Haitian Revolution being the best example of this. However, why did this situation apparently go unremarked in the case of Cangrejos and El Roble? It may have been because the concentration of military forces in the capital ensured the peace and because the mulattoes of Cangrejos constituted one of the capital's main defense forces. During the English invasion of 1797, the mulattoes of Cangrejos—the Cuerpo de Morenos—had volunteered to defend the capital.

26. Ibid., p. 123.

27. Ibid., p. 125.

28. Ibid., p. 125.

29. Ibid. Circular Número 255, 14 January 1812, p. 118.

30. Ibid.

31. Ibid.

32. Ibid.

33. Ibid.

34. Ibid.

35. Ibid.

36. Ibid. Carta Número 71, 14 January 1812, p. 117.

37. Ibid.

38. Ibid.

39. Ibid., número 75, p.127.

40. Ibid., número 75, p. 127.

41. Ibid., p. 130.

42. Ibid., p. 123.

43. Ibid., p. 130.

44. Philip S. Foner. *Historia de Cuba y sus relaciones con Estados Unidos,* p. 97.

Notes to Chapter III

45. *El proceso abolicionista en Puerto Rico:Documentos para su estudio.* Vol. I, p. 125.

46. The district of Bayamón, located to the north of Naranjito, to the west of Toa Alta and Toa Baja and to the east of Río Piedras, surrounds the bay of the Puerto Rican capital. Its land is flat and fertile and benefits from the waters of the Bayamón River, which flows into the bay of the capital. The river facilitated trade and the development of the sugar plantations.

47. Pierre Charles Gerard. *La economía haitiana y su vía de desarrollo.* Translated by María Teresa Moll (Mexico: Cuadernos Americanos, 1965), p. 38.

48. Lidio Cruz Monclova, *Historia de Puerto Rico*. Vol. I, Editorial Universitaria, 1970, p. 13.

49. Ibid., p. 82.

50. *El Investigador*. No. 2, February 1815, Vol. 16, p. 15. Colección Puertorriqueña, Universidad de Puerto Rico and AGPR, Fondo de los Gobernaderes, Estado de Población del Partido de Bayamón, 1820. Caja 243, E. 414.

51. Ibid.

52. AMB. Oficio Relativo a la Evación de Contribución del Hacendado Fernando Fernández, abril 1821, Folio 2, Caja 413.

53. Ibid.

54. Ibid.

55. AGPR. Fondo de los Gobernadores. Negociado y Seguridad Pública, Caja 370. Sumaria seguida contra los esclavos de Bayamón. Declaración de Ambrosio, 24 July 1821. Cayetano Náter.

56. Ibid. Ambrosio stated that Luis, a slave who was the *capataz* of the hacienda of Miguel Figueres had invited him to take part in the conspiracy. It was in fact Luis who informed him of the plans for the conspiracy.

57. Ibid.

58. Ibid.

59. Ibid.

60. Ibid.

61. Ibid. Informe del alcalde Cayetano Náter. 26 July 1821.

62. Ibid.

63. Ibid. Carta del Gobernador Arostegui. 29 February 1821.

64. Ibid. Carta de Cayetano Náter. 30 July 1821.

65. Ibid. Carta de Cayetano Náter. 25 July 1821.

66. So many suspects were arrested that the alcalde was obliged to send some of them to the capital. *Idem*. Carta de Cayetano Náter. 25 July 1821.

67. Ibid. Carta de Cayetano Náter. 8 August 1821.

68. Ibid. Carta de Francisco Igartúa (sic). 14 July 1821.

69. Ibid. Carta de Cayetano Náter. 25 July 1821.

70. Ibid. Carta de Cayetano Náter. Reservada, 24 July 1821.

71. Ibid. Carta de José C. Cardona. 26 July 1821.

72. Ibid. Carta de José C. Cardona. 26 July 1821.

73. Ibid. Carta de Francisco Alvarez. 10 August 1821.

74. Ibid. Carta de Arostegui. 21 August 1821.

75. Ibid. Carta de Cayetano Náter. 27 July 1821.

76. Ibid. Carta de Cayetano Náter. 13 August 1821.

77. Ibid. Sentencia, 15 August 1821. Mario and Narciso were executed on November 21 1821.

78. Real Cédula de su Majestad sobre la Educación, Trato y Ocupaciones de los Esclavos en todos sus dominios e Islas Filipinas, 1789. Legislación Ultramarina. Felipe Ontiveros. MDCCLX.

79. AHN. Sec. Ultramar, Legado 3313, Exp. 1, 23 February 1824. Miguel de la Torre. CIH Microfilms, UPR.

80. Ibid.

81. AGPR. Fondo de los Gobernadores. Seguridad Pública, Circular Suelta. 1824, Caja 59.

82. Ibid.

83. AGPR. Fondo de los Gobernadores, Caja 59. Negociado y Seguridad Pública. Carta de Santiago de Cardona, 4 July 1823.

84. AGPR. Fondo de los Gobernadores, Caja 59. Loose document dated 13 September 1826.

85. Ibid., 20 July 1826.

Notes to Chapter IV

86. AGPR. Fondo de los Gobernadores, Negocia do y Seguridad Pública 20 November 1823, Capitán Francisco Fernández de Castro. c. 371. Other documents about "Corsarios Insurgentes [Insurgent Corsairs] are in the same collection in cajas 371 and 374.

87. AGPR. Fondo Documental de los Gobernadores, Negociado y Seguridad Pública. 14 October 1822, Miguel de la Torre, c. 372.

88. AHN Ultramar, Legajo 5568. Exp. 15. No. 4, 1822. CIH Photocopies, UPR.

89. Ibid.

90. Lidio Cruz Monclova. *Historia de Puerto Rico*. Vol. I, p.122.

91. AGPR. Fondo Documental de los Gobernadores, Negociado y Seguridad. 14 October 1822, Miguel de la Torre, c. 374.

92. AGPR. Fondo de los Gobernadores, Negociado y Seguridad Pública, 18 September 1822, Miguel de la Torre, c. 374; 18 September 1822 and 19 de septiembre 1822. Federico Garcen, c. 374.

93. Ibid., and in AGPR, Fondo de los Gobernadores, Negociado y Seguridad Pública, 26 July 1821. Diputación Provincial, c. 374. Very detailed report about the military situation of the island in 1821.

94. The sugar boom is explained by the rise in raw sugar prices at the beginning of the nineteenth century. According to the 1821 census, in that year there were 28 wooden sugarmills and six iron ones in the district of Guayama. On the haciendas 173 cuerdas of cane were cultivated and peasant farmers grew 100 cuerdas of cane. In 1833 Guayama was the second most important producer and exporter of sugar cane in Puerto Rico.

95. "Infinitos africanos [Innumerable Africans]" was the phrase employed by Comandante Básquez at the time of the conspiracy to describe the presence of such a large number of *bozales* in this town. This document will be cited fully in contect later on.

96. AGPR. Fondo Documental de los Gobernadores, Negociado y Seguridad Pública, c. 372, Consejo de Guerra, Declaración de Juan Bautista Texidor; Idelfonso Vasallo, 30 September 1822.

97. Ibid.

98. AGPR. Fondo Documental de los Gobernadores, Negociado y Seguridad Pública, c. 372, Consejo de Guerra, Declaración de Francisco Cubelo; Idelfonso Vasallo, 30 September 1822.

99. Ibid.

100. AGPR. Fondo de los Gobernadores, Negociado y Seguridad Pública, c. 372, Declaración de Juan Lapre, 22 September 1822.

101. C. 373, Declaración de Mauricio, 22 September 1822.

102. Ibid.

103. AGPR. Fondo de los Gobernadores, Negociado y Seguridad Pública, c. 372, Declaración de Gustavo, 22 September 1822.

104. AGPR. Fondo de los Gobernadores, Negociado y Seguridad Pública, c. 372, Pedro Básquez, 21 September 1822.

105. Ibid.
106. Ibid.
107. AGPR. Fondo de los Gobernadores, Negociado y Seguridad Pública, c. 372, Consejo de Guerra, Declaración de José M Colón, 30 September 1822.
108. Ibid.
109. AGPR. Fondo de los Gobernadores, Negociado y Seguridad Pública, c. 372, Declaración de Francisco Cubelo, Confesión, 29 September 1822.
110. AGPR. Fondo de los Gobernadores, Negociado y Seguridad Pública, Idelfonso Vasallo, 39 September 1822.
111. Ibid.
112. CIH. Cajas Sueltas, Carta del Gobernador Gonzalo Linares, 22 September 1822.
113. AGPR. Fondo Municipal de Guayama. Libro de Actas del Ayuntamiento de Guayama (1820-1920) Marcelino Cintrón, Carta del 30 de septiembre de 1822, Acta del 7 de octubre 1822.
114. Ibid.
115. AGPR. Fondo de los Gobernadores, op. cit. 21 October 1822, Miguel García, c. 372.
116. AGPR., op. cit., 19 September 1822.
117. Cruz Monclova, Lidio. *Historia de Puerto Rico.* Vol. I, p. 141.
118. AGPR., op.cit. Alcaldía de Arecibo; 1 October 1822; Declaración de María Encarnación Montesinos. María Encarnación says that she does not know if she uttered those words as at the time she was drunk, on a fifth of rum and a little anisette for her stomach ailments; that if perchance she had caused offense a thousand pardons and that she spoke in jest to Nicolás Barriga about the feast of San Miguel.
119. Lidio Cruz Monclova. *Historia de Puerto Rico.* Vol. I, p. 141.
120. AGPR. Fondo Documental de los Goberrnadores. Angel Laborde al Excelentísimo Capitán General de la Isla de Puerto Rico, 17 November 1822. Seguridad Pública, caja 375.
121. Ibid.

Notes to Chapter V

122. Eduardo Newman Gandía. *Verdadera y auténtica historia de la Ciudad de Ponce*, pp. 260-261.
123. AGPR. Fondo de los Gobernadores. Censo y Riqueza; 1812 y 1822. Ponce.

124. Eduardo Newman Gandía, *op. cit.*, p. 261.

125. Ibid., p. 212.

126. O'Reylly. *Memorias*, p. 251; the free population consisted of 2,960 inhabitants in 1765. Eduardo Newman Gandía, p. 64, for the 1776 figures. AGPR. Censo y Riqueza, 1812. Fondos de los Gobernadores, 1812. AGPR. CLE. 19 Censo y Riqueza, March 1812. Fondo de los Gobernadores, 1821.Pedro T Córdova, *Memorias*, p. 255, Vol. II, 1826.

127. AGPR. Fondo de los Gobernadores. Licencias para la Introducción de esclavos, 5 June 1824, Miguel de la Torre.

128. Ibid.

129. Ibid.

130. *Gaceta Oficial de Puerto Rico,* 10 July 1826 and Pedro Tomás de Córdova, *Memorias*, pp. 106-7. The plans are described in the *Gaceta,* but the account of the events is that of Governor de la Torre, who traveled to Ponce and published his version in the newspaper on his return.

131. Eduardo Newman Gandío, *op. cit.* p. 261.

132. *Gaceta Oficial de Puerto Rico, op. cit.*

133. Ibid., p. 107. Newman Gandía points out that eleven of them were executed. These were: Francisco José, Antonio, Federico, Benito, Pablo Viejo, Ogui, José Félix and Faustino (from the Del Quemado hacienda), Francisco Antonio and Manuel, owned by Esteban Roque, and Inés, owned by Wedestein, p. 261.

134. Ibid., p. 109.

135. Ibid., p. 109.

136. *Real Cédula de su Majestad sobre la Educación, Trato y Ocupaciones de los Esclavos, en todos sus dominios e Islas Filipinas, 1789.* Legislación Ultramarina, MDCCLX.

137. *Reglamento sobre la Educación, Trato y Ocupaciones que deben dar a sus Esclavos los Dueños y Mayordomos en esta Isla [Rules respecting the education, treatment and occupations which slaveowners and overseers should give their slaves], 1826.* Miguel de la Torre, reprinted in Coll y Toste, ed. *Boletín histórico*, 10: 262-73.

138. Ibid. Capítulo V, Artículo II.

139. Ibid. Capítulo V, Artículo III.

140. Ibid., Capítulo VI, Artículo I.

141. Ibid., Capítulo VI, Artículo II.

142. Ibid., Capítulo VII, Artículo I.

143. Ibid., Capítulo VII, Artículo II.

144. Ibid., Capítulo VII, Artículo III.

145. Ibid., Capítulo VII, Artículo IV.

146. AGPR. Fondo de los Gobernadores, Circular 494, 30 July 1834; Pres. y Gobierno Capitán General de Puerto Rico; Caja 65, E. 23.

147. AGPR. Correspondencia de la Alcaldía Mayor del Distrito de Coamo, 29 December 1835, Coamo.

Notes to Chapter VI

148. Lidio Cruz Monclova, *Historia de Puerto Rico*, Vol. I, p. 81.

149. Ibid., p. 81.

150. Another factor that has been mentioned is the loan of 1 million pesos agreed by the Gobierno Superior de Puerto Rico to assist agriculture in general and in particular the sugar industry. Lidio Cruz Monclova, *Ibid.*, Vol. I, p. 194.

151. Balanza Mercantil de Puerto Rico, CIH. Microfilm, Universidad de Puerto Rico.

152. George Flinter. *Examen del estado actual de la esclavitud en Puerto Rico*, p. 179.

153. Balanza Mercantil, 1842, *op. cit.*

154. AHN Ultramar, Legajo 1070. Hacienda, Censo 1846. Clases de Establecimientos, valores y productos. CIH Microfilms.

155. Darío de Ormachea. "Memoria acerca de la Agricultura, el Comercio y las Rentas Internas de la Isla de Puerto Rico", 1847, in Coll y Toste, ed. *Boletín Histórico de Puerto Rico*, Vol. II, p. 226.

156. Ibid., p. 226.

157. The mills were originally made of wood, but later they were made from iron. For an excellent description of the technical development of a sugar plantation on the island in the mid-nineteenth century, see Andrés Ramos Mattei, *Los libros de cuentas de la Hacienda Mercedita.* CEREP.

158. James Bandinell. *Some Accounts of the Trade of Slaves from Africa* (London: Longmans, 1842), p. 148. For the history of the slave trade in Puerto Rico, see Arturo Morales Carrión, *Auge y decadencia de la trata negrera (1820-1860),* Centro de Estudios Avanzados de Puerto Rico y el Caribe, Instituto de Cultura Puertorriqueña, 1978.

159. Some examples may be found in AGPR, Real Audiencia, Real Acuerdo, 6 March 1836, Caja 4, 1836-7; Consulado de Francia, Asuntos Comerciales, número 10. Puerto Rico, 30 May 1827, in the *Proceso abolicionista de Puerto Rico,* p. 8-9.

160. AGPR. Carta de Juan B. Bertrés al Excelentísimo Gobernador de Puerto Rico, 22 February 1847. F. 3. Political & Civil Affairs, Fondo de los Gobernadores, Caja 23, Entry 66. The theme of free vs enslave labor is

extremely well covered in José Curet, *De la esclavitud a la abolición*, CEREP, 1979.

161. Ibid.

162. Ibid.

163. AGPR. Carta de Constantino Souteyran al Excelentísimo Gobernaod de Puerto Rico, 3 March 1847. Political & Civil Affairs, Caja 23, Entry 66. Fondo de los Gobernadores.

164. Ibid.

165. Leopoldo Krugg, PRG Foreign Office, Series 84, Vol. 1263, pp. 133-138, V, Feb 6, 1866. *El proceso abolicionista en Puerto Rico: documentos para su studio.* Vol. I: "La institución de la esclavitud y su crisis, 1823-1873", CIH. San Juan, Puerto Rico, 1974.

166. Arthur Cole. *Wholesale, Commodity Prices in the United States, 1700-1801.*

167. AHN. Ultramar. Legajo 1074, 29. Hacienda, febrero 1847. Microfilm CIH, Universidad de Puerto Rico.

168. AHN. Ultramar. Legajo 1070, 88, 15 February 1845. Microfilm, CIH, Universidad de Puerto Rico.

169. AHN. Ultramar. Legajo 1069, Gobernador Méndez Vigo, 14 December 1843. Microfilm, CIH, Universidad de Puerto Rico.

170. Lidio Cruz Monclova, *op. cit.*, p. 264.

171. AHN. Ultramar. Legajo 1074, Oficio 22. Reporte del Ministerio de Hacienda, 18 August 1846. Microfilm, CIH, Universidad de Puerto Rico.

172. Darío Ormachea, *Memorias, op. cit.,* p. 421.

173. Rubén Carbonel. "Compraventas de esclavos en San Juan 1817-1873". Unpublished thesis. Departamento de Historia, Universidad de Puerto Rico.

174. AGPR. Fondo de Guyama. Libro de Actas, 2 March 1843 y Balanza Mercantil de Puerto Rico, nota núm. 3, 1 October 1844.

Notes to Chapter VII

175. The sixth one occurred in 1832 in the district of Vega Baja at Ramón Soler's hacienda. This will be discussed in Chapter IX, which deals with Vega Baja.

176. AMP. Circular Núm. 118, Caja 17; Correspondencia del Excelentísimo Gobernador 1828-1829, 16 December 1828.

177. AMP. 21 January 1833; Oficio 1832-1837 Núm. 8, Caja Núm. 8.

178. Ibid.

179. AMP Oficios (1835-1836); 17 April 1835; Núm. 176-2, Caja 17.

180. AMP Oficios Núm. 132 (1836-1837); 5 October 1835, Caja 17.

181. This revolt was the result of the town's priest who encouraged his slaves to light a fire at the foot of the plaque commemorating the foundation of the town. AGPR, 30 de Julio de 1830, Negociado y Seguridad, Caja Núm. 371.

182. AMP. Oficios Núm. 1839, 13 August 1839, Núm. 203, Caja 17.

183. AHN. Ultramar, Legajo 5066/20, Núm. 2. López de Baño, 26 September 1840.

184. Microfilm, CIH, Universidad de Puerto Rico. Fondo de los Gobernadores. Without having had access to the municipal archives of Guayanilla, the description of what happened makes this section very superficial. The description of the conspiracy is taken from a note sent by Governor López de Baño to the Regency in Spain.

185. Ibid.

186. Ibid.

187. AGPR. Fondo de los Gobernadores. Pasaportes, Caja Núm. 151, 20 January 1841.

188. AHN. Legajo 5066/20, Núm. 2, *op. cit.*

189. Ibid.

190. AHN. Ultramar, Legajo 5066/21; 28 October 1841, Núm. 1, Carta Núm. 42, López de Baño

191. Ibid.

192. Ibid.

193. Ponce was the district where the greatest number of slave conspiracies in Puerto Rico took place (1800-1873). The conspiracies occurred on July 10, 1826; January 21, 1833; April 7, 1835; October 5, 1836 and August 17, 1836. Although they were all unsuccessful, they prepared the way for the conspiracy of December 1841.

194. AHN. Legajo 1069, Exp. 22, CIH, Universidad de Puerto Rico.

195. AGPR. AMG. Libro de Actas, 2 March 1843.

196. AGPR. Fondo Documental de los Gobernadores. Political & Civil Affairs, Primera Pieza. Proceso formado contra varios negros acusados de estar comprendidos en una conspiración para asesinar a los blancos e incendiar este pueblo, que fue descubierta el 18 de diciembre de 1841. Fiscal, el Capitán de Infantería Antonio Fortuño; Escribano, Sargento Pedro Mayor. Caja 375.

We have reconstructed the conspiracy based on the statement of Marcos, the slave who betrayed it, and statements that emerged following the official inquiry into the incident as they appear in the criminal evidence cited above, Folios 2 and 3.

197. Ibid. Declaración de Isidoro. Folios 4, 5, 6. In this statement Isidoro says that details of the conspiracy were given to him by Thelemaco, a slave of Juan Castaño.

198. Ibid. Thelemaco's statement reconfirmed this statement.

199. Ibid. Declaración de Thelemaco. Folios 11, 12, and 13.

200. Ibid. Declaración de Isidoro.

201. Ibid.

202. Ibid. Declaración de Marcos, "el delator [informer."

203. AMP. Caja 17, 28 January 1842. Luis Font. He was accused of appropriating part of the *subsidio* intended for the treasuries.

204. Ibid. Declaración de Alejandro, esclavo de José Castaño.

205. Ibid. Declaración de Thelemaco.

206. Ibid. Declaración de Isidoro.

207. Ibid.

208. Ibid. Declaración de Marcos.

209. AHN. Carta de Rafael de Sevilla al Secretario de Estado y del Despacho de Marina y Comercio y Gobernación. 23 December 1841, Legajo 5066/7. Photocopy in CIH.

210. Ibid.

211. AHN Ultramar, Legajo 5066/29, Carta Núm. 245; Carta de Rafael de Sevilla a Méndez Vigo, 23 December 1845. Photocopy in CIH, Universidad de Puerto Rico.

212. AHN Ultramar, Legajo 5066/7. Carta de Méndez Vigo. 23 December 1841. Photocopy, CIH, Universidad de Puerto Rico.

213. AHN Ultramar. Legajo 5066/29, Carta Núm. 245, Méndez Vigo, 7 January 1842. CIH, Filmillas B-LXXV-1-b and B-LXXV-1C. Universidad de Puerto Rico.

214. AGPR. "Proceso Formado", Pieza Criminal. Carta de Rafael de Sevilla. 27 December 1841. Fondo Documental de los Gobernadores.

215. AMP, dated 29 December 1841, Caja Núm. 17. At the time of consulting this document, it had not been classified in this archive.

216. AMP. 27 December 1841. Departamento militar de Ponce núm. 203, Caja 81. Loose document.

217. AHN Legajo 5066/29. Carta Núm. 245, 17 January 1842; Santiago Méndez Vigo. Photocopy, CIH.

218. Ibid.

219. Ibid.

220. AGPR. 6 February 1842. Carta de Rafael de Sevilla a Méndez Vigo. Fondo Documental de los Gobernadores, Asuntos varios, Caja 144.

221. Ibid.

222. Ibid.

Notes to Chapter VIII

223. Tomás Pamias, from the district of Aguadilla, had bought La Esperanza in 1829. "It had over 400 *cuerdas*, sugar factories, a residence and livestock when Pamias bought it 1829". Protocolos Notariales de Isabela, 1 September 1829, p. 72.

224. AHN Sec. Ultramar. Legajo 5068, Exp. 29, Doc. 2. Declaración de Pamias en *El proceso abolicionista, op. cit.,* p. 159.

225. Ibid. p. 160.

226. Ibid. Declaración del párroco Román, p. 154.

227. Ibid. Declaración de Cesáreo Zeno, p. 147.

228. There is evidence confirming Garabaín's dubious reputation. A. Román points out in his statement that Garabaín arrived in Isabela a bankrupt. Zeno had to point out in his summary that Garabaín had never exceeded the limits of his powers and later Governor Méndez Vigo had to call for an investigation into his conduct.

229. Concerning the education, treatment and occupations that the owners and *mayordomos* should provide for their slaves, Article III, Chapter II states the following: "On Sundays and holidays, both days of obligation, the hacienda owners should make the slaves who are already baptized hear mass and the explanation of Christian doctrine; they shall not employ any in the tasks of the hacienda, but they may exercise them for two hours as specified by the owner or steward, to sweep and clean the houses and workshops and for even longer when it is necessary to harvest crops and perform other urgent duties."

230 AHN. Legajo 5068. Declaración del párroco Román, p. 154.

231. Ibid., p. 155.

232. Ibid., p. 144.

233. Ibid., p. 143.

234. Ibid. Declaración de Pamias, p. 161.

235. Ibid.

236. Ibid. Declaración de Mateu, p. 157.

237. Ibid. Declaración del párroco Román, p. 155. The priest stated that he had seen everything from his residence: "and looking out of a window that gave onto the streets."

238. Ibid.

239. Ibid. Declaración de José Esteban, p. 162.

240. Ibid.

241. Ibid., p. 164.

242. Ibid. Declaración de Anacleto Batista, p. 165.

243. Ibid., p. 165.

Notes to Chapter IX

244. Fray Iñigo Abbad, *Historia geográfica...*, op. cit., p. 127.

245. Juana Gil Bermejo García. *Panorama histórico de la agricultura en Puerto Rico*. Seville: Instituto de Cultura Puertorriqueña, 1970, p. 128. This source mentions Quinlan, providing him as an example of those English people who gave a considerable boost to the sugar economy.

246. Fray Iñigo Abbad, *Historia geográfica...*, op. cit., p. 122.

247. Ibid.

248. Ibid.

249. Ibid., p. 153, and FDG in AGPR, Serie: Municipios, Sub Serie Toa Baja; Exp. Planilla de 1812, Caja 587.

250. Ibid.

251. Ibid.

252. AGPR, Fondo de los Gobernadores, Serie: Municipios, Sub Serie Toa Baja; Exp. Acta del Ayuntamiento de 11 January 1813, Caja 588.

253. Pedro Tomás de Córdova. *Memorias geográficas, históricas y estadísticas de la Isla de Puerto Rico*. 6 vols. San Juan: Instituto de Cultura Puertorriqueña, Vol. II, p. 71.

254. Ibid.

255. AGPR, Fondo de los Gobernadores, Serie: Municipios, Sub Serie Toa Baja, Exp. Lista de Contribuyentes—1829, Caja 588.

256. Ibid.

257. Pedro Tomás de Córdova, *op. cit.*, 1, p. 71.

258. FDG in AGPR, Serie: Asuntos Políticos y Civiles, Sub Serie Visitas, Caja 189.

259. Ibid.

260. Generoso Morales Muñoz. *Fundación del Pueblo de Cataño*, San Juan: Talleres Gráficos de la Imprenta Venezuela, 1946, pp. 43-45.

261. Ibid.

262. AGPR, Protocolos Notariales, Toa Baja, Otros Funcionarios, 1838-1842, f. 6, caja 572.

263. Ibid., f. 7.

264. AGPR., Fondo Documental: Obras Públicas, Serie: Obras Municipales, Legajo 66, Exp. 1, Caja 346. When it split from the town of Dorado, Toa Baja lost the quarters of Dorado, Mameyal, Iguillar, Maguayo, Espinosa and (Río?) Lajas.

265. Archivo Histórico de Madrid, Sección: Ultramar, Exp. 117, L. 1070. "Censo de 1846: Clase de Establecimientos; sus valores y productos". Photocopy in the Centro de Investigaciones Históricas de la Universidad de Puerto Rico.

266. Universidad de Puerto Rico, Colección Puertorriqueña. "Real Cédula aboliendo el tráfico de negros", Madrid, *Gaceta Oficial de Puerto Rico,* 19 December 1817.

267. AGPR, Fondo de Gobernadores, Serie: Municipios, Sub Serie Toa Baja, Exp. Extranjeros, Caja 588.

268. AGPR, Protocolos Notariales for the years 1836 to 1843 in Toa Baja.

269. Individual escapes were the most common form of protest against the institution of slavery throughout Puerto Rico as well as in Toa Baja. We include some of those recorded in the *Gaceta Oficial de Puerto Rico*:

    1. 21 June 1820   — 1 slave of Santiago Ríos
    2. 25 September 1822   — 1 slaves of Santiago Ríos
    3. 26 October 1822   — 1 slave of Santiago Córdova
    4. 4 October 1824   — 2 slaves of Ramón Quinlan
    5. 13 January 1838   — 1 slave of Juan Hernández
    6. 6 February 1840   — 1 slave from El Plantaje
    7. 14 July 1840   — 1 slave from El Plantaje

270. AGPR, Fondo de Gobernadores, Serie: Agencias Gubernamentales, Sub Serie Seguridad Pública, Exp. Interrogatorio de Ambrosio, esclavo de Miguel Figueres, 1821, Caja 370.

271. Ibid.

272. AGPR, Fondo de Gobernadores, Serie: Asuntos Políticos y Civiles, Sub Serie Esclavos (negros-libertos), 1799-1825, Caja 59.

273. Ibid.

274. Ibid.

275. Ibid.

276. AGPR, Fondo de Gobernadores: Serie: Agencias Gubernmentales, Sub Series Seguridad Pública, Exp. Sumario contra el Negro Pablo de la propiedad de Francisco Cantero, iniciado en la sublevación que tuvo lugar en Toa Baja la noche del 26 al 27 abril 1843, Caja 375.

277. Ibid.

278. AGPR, Protocolos Notariales, Toa Baja, 1839, Otro Funcionarios, f. 97-98, Caja I 752.

279. AGPR, Fondo de Gobernadores, Serie: Agencias Gubernamentales, Sub Serie Seguridad Pública, Exp. Comandante Militar del primer departamento..., Caja 375.

280. Ibid.

281. Ibid.

282. Ibid.

283. Ibid.

284. Ibid.

285. AGPR, Fondo de Gobernadores, Serie: Asuntos Gubernamentales, Sub Serie Seguridad Pública, Exp. Incidentes y disposiciones concernientes a la sublevación..., Caja 375.

286. Ibid.

287. Ibid. Oficio del Publo de Loíza de 6 abril 1843.

288. Ibid. Exp. Defensa de Toa Baja contra la sublevación de negros esclavos...All the decorations are listed in this document.

Notes to Chapter X

289. AMP, Circular Núm. 389, 1847; David Laporte, Alcalde Ponce, Caja 10 (Según Ordenación de 1974).

290. Ibid.

291. Ibid.

292. Ibid.

293. Ibid.

294. AMP. Copiador de Oficios en correspondencia con el Capitán General y el Superintendente de la Isla. 29 May 1848, Núm. 446, Caja 17.

295. Ibid.

296. Balanza Mercantil, 1849.

297. AHN. Legajo 5069, Oficio 3-6; Gobierno y Capitanía General de Puerto Rico, Carta 98, July 1848. CIH.

298. Ibid.

299. Ibid.

300. Bando de Policia y Buen Gobierno del General Prim. 31 May 1848. CIH. Photocopy.

301. Ibid.

302. Ibid.

303. Apéndice al Bando de Prim. 9 June 1848. CIH. Photocopy.

304. Ibid.

305. Ibid.

306. AMP. Documento suelto, 12 November 1844. it states that "the slaves were forced to watch the punishment of José de los Santos". Oficios 1844-1845. Núm. 290.

307. AMP. Documento suelto, 21 July 1845. Caja 17.

308. AMP. Documento suelto, 11 July 1848, Caja 17. David Laporte, Oficios al Capitán General y Superintendente de la Isla, Núm. 19.

309. Ibid.

310. AMP. Documento suelto, 15 July 1848; Oficios del Capitán General y Superintendente de la Isla de Puerto Rico, Núm. 20 y Núm. 447.

311. *Gaceta Oficial de Puerto Rico*, 29 July 1848.

312. Sub-secretario y Ministro de Guerra, 18 July 1848.

313. *Idem* and AHN. Legajo 5068/22. Núm. 1; Dirección del Gobierno de Ultramar, Núm. 21, 7 August 1848.

314. AGPR, Testimonio de la primera pieza de los Autos de Residencia de don Juan Prim, Capitán General de la Isla de Puerto Rico y Preisdente de la Audiencia. 30 October 1848, Folios 258-264.

315. Ibid.

Notes to Chapter XI

316. AMVB, Censo de Esclavos, 8 June 1833; Censo de Esclavos, 1837.

317. Apparently Soler purchased his lands in several transactions. For example, in 1830 he bought 330 *cuerdas* from ten small landowners. Ramón Soler was the brother of the other Toa Baja Solers, who are referred to later.

318. AMVB. 48F, Exp. 3, Caja 1839, Planilla Agrícola 1838.

319. Idem.

320. AMVB. 67F, Exp. 7, Caja 1839; Censo de Esclavos, 1838.

321. AMVB. Exp. 5, Caja 1839; Planilla Agrícola, 1838.

322. AMVB, Caja 1839; Censo de Esclavos, 1838.

323. AMVB. 67F, Exp. 7, Caja 1839; Planilla Agrícola, 1838.

324. AMVB. Exp. 5, Caja 1839; Censo de Esclavos, 1838

325. AMVB. 67F, Exp. 7, 71F,Caja 1839; Planilla Agrícola, 1838.

326. AMVB. Exp. 5, Caja 1838; Censo de Esclavos, 1838

327. AMVB. 4 of. Exp. 12, Caja 1848; Censo de Esclavos, 1847.

328. AMVB. 4 of. Exp. 12, Caja 1848; Censo de Esclavos, 1847.

329. Ibid.

330. AMVB. Libro de Actas del Ayuntamiento, Caja 1841, 8 January 1843.

331. AMVB. Libro de Actas del Ayuntamiento, Caja 1841, 22 July 1840.

332. AMVB. Libro de Actas del Ayuntamiento, Caja 1841; 21 March 1841 and Libro de Actas del Ayuntamiento de Vega Baja, 8 January 1843.

333. AMVB. Libro de Actas (II), 12 June 1837, Caja 1838. "Soler mistreats his slaves" was the phrase used by the Ayuntamiento in the Libro de Actas of 8 January 1843.

334. AMM. Legajo Núm. 59, Registro 2051-2068; Correspondence de la Administración Local y Gobierno.

335. AMVB. Libro de Actas II; 27 May 1837.

336. AMVB. Libro de Actas; 16 October 1841.

337. Agustín Otero was the owner of a small sugar hacienda in the Barrio

Algarrobo of Vega Baja where he had fourteen slaves. He was also the agent of the hacienda belonging to Antonio Dávila. As its manager, he became involved in litigation about title deeds with the neighbour Peroza, who alleged that the Dávila heirs had taken lands belonging to him.

338. AGPR. Fondo Documental de los Gobernadores, Fiscal Affairs, Negros; 113-114, 12 July 1845. Declaración de José Miguel.

339. Ibid.

340. Ibid.

341. CIH. Legajo 5068/29, Núm. 1; Ultramar, 26 August 1849. Ministro de la Gobernación del Reino and *Gaceta Oficial de Puerto Rico*, 29 August 1848.

342. *Gaceta Oficial de Puerto Rico*, 29 August 1848.

343. Ibid.

344. Ibid.

345. Ibid.

Notes to Chapter XII

346. AGPR. Protocolos Notariales, Naguabo, 1822. F. 22.

347. See Chapter IV.

348. AGPR. Protocolos Notariales de Humacao. Testamento de Guillermo Bedlow, 1834, p. 72.

349. AGPR. Protocolos Notariales; Compraventa de Esclavos, Naguabo, 1842.

350. Ibid.

351. AHN. Legajo 5063, 40.1-2 and 5, Ministro de Marina; 21 January 1843. CIH Photocopy.

352. Ibid.

353. Ibid.

354. AGPR. Fondo Documental de los Gobernadores. Caja 61, Several transactions dated September 4, 1824; June 8, 1824 and May 12, 1824.

355. Ibid.

356. This means that he paid four pesos less per person than the eight pesos previously paid.

357. AHN. Legajo 5066. Capitanía General de Puerto Rico. Carta 333-335, 28 April 1846.

358. Ibid. Reporte de Juan Topete; 28 April 1841.

359. Ibid.

360. Ibid.

361. AHN Ultramar. Expediente sobre Criminalidad en Puerto Rico; 18

July 1870. *El proceso abolicionista*. Doc. 48, p. 173; and AGPR. Documentos del Presidio Provincial de Puerto Rico.

362. In an unpublished monograph by María Calderón, *La Hacienda "La Califonia"*, she points out that in 1862, La California, despite its modern machinery, was experiencing a precarious economic situation. It was heavily indebted and plagued by problems. In 1864, Carlos Curet took on his brother to manage the La California. Carlos authorized him to give the person of his choice the job of mayordomo. He chose José María Colón. Years later he sold the hacienda to him.

363. AGPR. Presidio Provincial de Puerto Rico, 274. Hoja Penal del confinado Gil, esclavo de don Domingo Curet; 25 November 1868. Their ages were as follows: Vicente, 24-25 years; Juan Pablo, 25-26; Primo, 26-28; José, 22-24 and Gil, 16-17. All of them had been born in Africa.

364. Ibid.

365. Ibid.

366. Ibid.

367. Ibid. Primo and José were also forced to witness the execution of their companions. They were sentenced to wearing a large ring around their necks and they had to provide compensation for life to Rosario Colón, the overseer's sister.

368. Dirección de Administración Número 367. Reservado. Laureano Sanz; 1 March 1870. *El proceso abolicionista*, p. 174.

369. Some of the most important observations are as follows: the alcaldía of Guayama pointed out that the rising criminality was due to the increase in population or the state of poverty in which the island existed; the alcaldía of San Francisco indicates that ignorance is the main cause of the said crimes; the alcaldía of Arecibo points out that the very nature of the island's countryside provided the frugal labourer with everything required to meet his needs; the alcaldía mayor of Catedral pointed out that it was the lack of morality, that is, the fact that marriage was rare; the alcaldía of Mayagüez attributes the problem to the lack of credit and banking which do not allow the haciendas to develop and therefore leave the workers without employment, and the Alcaldía of San Germán also attributes it to the rise in vagrancy, but that of the day laborers.

Notes to Chapter XIII

370. These conclusions are based on a preliminary study of runaways for which we used information taken from the *Gaceta Oficial de Puerto Rico*.

371. AGI. Legajo 6375, Ultramar, Carta reservada Núm. 2; Gobernador

Ramón de Castro a su Majestad. 22 January 1795.

372. AHN. Documentos Españoles A.XL-VII, 8-d, (Microfilm in CIH). *El proceso abolicionista, op. cit.*, p. 124.

373. AMM. Carta de Toribio Montes, Núm. 37; Ayuntamiento de Manatí, Reg. Núm. 1812. 3 November 1805.

374. AGPR. Fondo Documental de los Gobernadores, Seguridad Públca, 14 October 1822, Caja 372.

375. AGPR. Alcaldía Mayor del Distrito de Coamo; 29 December 1835, Coamo.

376. Angel de Barrios Román. *Antropología socioeconómica en el Caribe*, Editora Quisqueyana, 1974; p. 99.

377. AGPR. Fondo Documental de los Gobernadores, Revolución de Lares, 29 September 1868, Caja 180.

378. AGPR. Fondo Documental de los Gobernadores, Revolución de Lares, Piezas 1-3, Caja 176.

379. Ibid.

380. AGPR. Fondo Documental de los Gobernadores; *Doc. Cit.*, 24 September 1868. Andrés Dapena, Añasco and 6 November 1868, Joaquín Dapena.

381. Ibid. Manuel Corrada, 25 September 1868 and another statement by Manuel Corrada of 28 September 1868.

382. Ibid. Alcaldía de Guayama, 13 November 1868.

383. Ibid. Relación nominal de los reos comprendidos en los diversos partidos de que consta el procedimiento instruido por motivo de la rebellion de Lares y otras jurisdicciones con mención de su naturaleza y vecindad; Caja 485-486.

384. AGPR. AMG. Libro de Actas; March 2, 1843.

385. AGPR. Fondo Documental de los Gobernadores: Seguridad Pública, Sumario contra el negro Pablo; May 22, 1843. C. 375.

386. AGPR. Fondo Documental, Obras Públicas. Miguel de la Torre; January 10, 1832. Los de días de San Miguel.

387. Bando del General Prim Contra la Raza Africana, 1848.

388. AGPR. Fondo Documental. Presidio Provincial de Puerto Rico, Caja 274. There are several files about this case, and AHN, Ultramar; Expediente sobre Criminalidad, in *El proceso abolicionista*, p. 173.

389. Alejandro Tapia y Rivera says the same thing in *Mis memorias*; in Fernández Méndez, ed. *Crónicas de Puerto Rico*, p. 476; but adds that "Some killed an capataz who became loathed on account of his harsh and cruel behaviour in order to ensure the gallows as the only end to their misfortunes."

Glossary

Alcalde	municipal officer with administrative and judicial functions
Alcalde mayor	local chief magistrate and administrative officer of a province
alcaldía mayor	magistrate court's Administrative division ruled by an alcalde mayor
Alguacil	constable or peace officer
Alguacil mayor	councilman and principal government officer
Arroba	measure equivalent to 25 pounds of sugar
Auditor de guerra	judge-advocate of the army; audiencia judge responsible for army affairs
Ayuntamiento	municipal government; the cabildo (city council)
Bohío	hut made of palm branches with thatched roof
Bomba	songs and dance music with a traditional African rhythm
Bozal, bozales	African-born slaves and laborers
Camino real	high road
Capataz	overseer
Casa real	principal building of a town
Cazadores	light infantry
Cédula de gracia	royal charter
Cédula real	royal decree or order
Coartación	self-manumission
Colono	sugar planter
Comisario de guerra	official in charge of fiscal matters relating to the army
Conuco	small holding

Corregidores	chief magistrate
Cortes	Parliament; the senate and congress of deputies of Spain
Cuartillo	measurement
Cuerda	unit of land = 0.97 acre
Escribano	notary
Fiscal	public prosecutor
Gobierno de Ultramar	Royal Overseas Government
Hacendado	landowning country gentleman
Hacienda	great landed estate, usually processing its own sugar cane or coffee
Hato	large expanse of land without fixed fences or boundaries used for raising animals
Ladino	in contradistinction to *Bozal*, a Black person born in Africa but able to speak Spanish, and supposedly introduced before the slave trade was prohibited
Liberto	freed slave, as opposed to one born free
Macuquina	Spanish colonial coinage
Mayordomo	foreman; overseer on a plantation
Moreno	free Black person
Nación	nation, or ethnic group to which Africans belong
Pardo	mulatto; a person of mixed blood
Peso fuertes	20 reales
Quintal	measure equivalent to 100 lbs.

Real	the most widely used denomination of Spanish American coinage; eight reales were equal to one peso.
Regidor	city councilman; member of the ayuntamiento
Sargento mayor	second-in-command of the urban militias; in frontier areas, often a non-professional in command of local forces under the lieutenant captain-general
Sindico procurador	attorney or official in charge of the military draft
Subsidio	tax on personal wealth for the haciendas
Teniente de guerra	representative of the governor
Trapiche	mill that grinds the sugar cane
Trapiche de sangre	primitive sugar mill producing muscovado sugar

Bibliography

Books

Acosta y Calvo, José Julián. *La servidumbre en Puerto Rico*. San Juan, Puerto Rico: Impr. de Sancerret, 1873.

Bandinell, James. *Some Accounts of the Trade in Slaves from Africa*. London: Longman, 1842.

Baralt, Guillermo et al. *El Machete de Ogún: Las luchas de los esclavos en Puerto Rico (siglo XIX)*. Río Pedras, Puerto Rico: CEREP, Proyecto de Divulgación Popular, 1990.

Bernal, Calixto. *Apuntes sobre la cuestión de la reforma política y de la introducción de africanos en las islas de Cuba y Puerto Rico*. Madrid: Est. Tipográfico de T. Tortanet, 1856.

Cepero-Bonilla, Raúl. *Azúcar y abolición*. Havana: Instituto Cubano del Libro, Editorial de Ciencias Sociales, 1971.

Cifre de Loubriel, Estela. *La inmigración en Puerto Rico durante el siglo XIX*. San Juan: Instituto de Cultura Puertorriqueña, 1964.

Cochin, Agustín. *L'Espagne et l'esclavage dans iles de Cuba et de Porto Rico*. Paris: J. Claye, Imp., 1869.

Cole, Arthur. *Wholesale Commodity Prices in the United States, 1700-1861*, 2 vols. Cambridge, Mass.: Harvard University and International Scientific Committee on Price History, 1938. Reprinted 1969 [2 vols. in 1].

Coll y Toste, Cayetano. *Historia de la esclavitud en Puerto Rico. Información y documentos*. Compiled by Isabel Cuchí Coll. 2nd ed. San Juan: Sociedad de Autores Puertorriqueños, 1972.

Cordero, Michel. *La Revolución Haitiana y Santo Domingo*. Santo Domingo: Editorial Nacional D.N., 1968.

Córdova, Pedro Tomás de. *Memorias geográficas, históricas, económicas y estádisticas de la Isla de Puerto Rico*, 6 vols. Mexico: Editorial Coqui, 1968.

Corwin, Arthur. *Spain and the Abolition of Slavery in Cuba, 1817-1866*. Austin: University of Texas Press, 1967.

Cruz Monclova, Lidio. *Historia de Puerto Rico.* 6 vols. San Juan: Editorial Universitaria, 1970.

Curet, José. *De las esclavitud a la abolición: transiciones económicas en las haciendas azucareras de Ponce, 1845-1873.* San Juan, Puerto Rico: CEREP, 1979.

_____. *Los Amos hablan: unas conversaciones entre un esclavo y su amo, aparecidas en el Ponceño, 1852-53.* Río Piedras, Puerto Rico: Editorial Cultural, 1986.

Davis, H. P. *Black Democracy—The Story of Haiti.* New York: Lincoln MacVeagh Vial Press, 1928.

Díaz Soler, Luis. *Historia de la esclavitud negra en Puerto Rico (1493-1890).* 2nd ed. Río Piedras, Puerto Rico: Editorial Universitaria, 1965.

Ely, Roland T. *Cuando reinaba su majestad el azúcar.* Buenos Aires: Editorial Sudamericana, 1963.

Esclavos prófugos y cimarrones: Puerto Rico, 1770-1870. Edición, estudio preliminar y notas de Benjamín Nistal Moret. Río Piedras, Puerto Rico: Editorial de la Universidad de Puerto Rico, 1984.

Fernández Méndez, Eugenio, ed. *Crónicas de Puerto Rico desde la conquista hasta nuestros días.* 3 vols. San Juan, Puerto Rico: Editorial Universitaria, 1970.

Ferrer de Couto, José. *Los negros en sus diversos estados y condiciones tales como son, cómo se suponen que son y cómo deben ser.* 2nd ed. New York: Imp. De Hallet, 1864.

Figueroa, Loida. *Breve historia de Puerto Rico.* Río Piedras, Puerto Rico: Edil, Inc., 1969.

Figueroa, Luis A. *Sugar, Slavery, and Freedom in Nineteenth-Century Puerto Rico.* Chapel Hill: University of North Carolina Press, 2005.

Flinter, George Dawson. *Examen del estado actual de los esclavos de la isla de Puerto Rico bajo el gobierno español.* New York: Imp. Española del Redactor, 1832.

_____. *Travels to the West Indies With Notice About Cuba and Puerto Rico.* London: Longman, 1840.

Foner, Philip. *Historia de Cuba y sus Relaciones con Estados Unidos.* Translated by Raquel Catalá. 2 vols. Havana: Instituto Cubano del Libro, Editorial de Ciencias Sociales, 1973.

Franco, J. L. *Historia de la Revolución de Haití.* Havana: Academia de
   Ciencias de Cuba, 1966.
Gandía, Eduardo N. *Benefactores y hombres notables de Puerto Rico.*
   2 vols. Ponce, Puerto Rico: Imprenta Liston, 1899.
Garrido, Roque E. *Historia documentada de la Conspiración de los
   Soles y Rayos de Bolívar.* 2 vols. Havana: Imprenta El Siglo XX,
   1929.
Genovese, Eugene. *In Red and Black.* New York: Vintage Books,
   1971.
Gérard, Pierre C. *La economía haitiana y su vía de desarrollo.* Mexico:
   Cuadernos Americanos, 1965.
Gil Bermejo, Juan. *Panorama histórico de la agricultura en Puerto
   Rico.* Seville: Instituto de Cultura Puertorriqueña, 1970.
Gómez Acevedo, Labor. *Organización y reglamentación de trabajo en
   el Puerto Rico del siglo XIX.* San Juan: Instituto de Cultura
   Puertorriqueña, 1970.
Goveia, Elsa. *Slave Society in the British Leeward Islands at the end of
   the Eighteenth Century.*
Cambridge, Mass: Murray Printing Press. Published in the Caribbean
   by the Institute of Caribbean Studies, 1965.
Guerra y Sánchez, R. *Sugar and Slavery in the Caribbean.* New
   Haven: Yale University Press, 1964.
Hall, Gwendolyn Midlo. *Social Control in Slave Plantation Societies:
   A Comparison of St. Domingue and Cuba.* Baltimore: Johns
   Hopkins Press, 1973.
Kelley, J., and F. Harris. *Black Separation and the Caribbean 1860.*
   Edited by Howard Bele. Ann Arbor: University of Michigan Press,
   1970.
Klein, Herbert. *Slavery in the Americas: A Comparative Study of
   Virginia and Cuba.* Chicago: University of Chicago Press, 1968.
Knight, Franklin. *Slave Society in Cuba during the Nineteenth
   Century.* Madison: University of Wisconsin Press, 1970.
Labra y Cadraña, Rafael María de. *La abolición de la esclavitud en las
   Antillas españolas.* Madrid: Imprenta J. E. Morete, 1869.
_____. *La abolición de la esclavitud en el orden económico.* Madrid:
   Imprenta de J. Nogueras, 1873.
Larrazabal, Blanco E. *Los negros y la esclavitud en Santo Domingo.*

Santo Domingo: Julio Pango e Hijos, 1967.

Le Riverend, Julio. *Historia económica de Cuba*. Barcelona: Ediciones Ariel, 1972.

Madden, Robert. *A Twelve Month Residence in the West Indies*. Vol. 1. Philadelphia: Carey, Lea and Blanchard, 1935.

Mannix, D., and M. Cowley. *Historia de la trata de negros*. Madrid: Alianza Editorial, 1968.

Mayo Santana, Raúl et al. *Cadenas de esclavitud—y de solidaridad: esclavos y libertos en San Juan, siglo XIX*. San Juan, Puerto Rico: Centro de Investigaciones Sociales, Universidad de Puerto Rico, 1997.

Ministerio de Ultramar, Spain. *Disposiciones sobre la repression y castigo del tráfico negrero*. Madrid: Imp. Nacional, 1886.

Morales Carrión, Arturo. *Puerto Rico and the Non-Hispanic Caribbean*. Río Piedras, Puerto Rico: Editorial Universitaria, 1971.

Morales y Morales, Vidal. *Iniciadores y primeros mártires de la Revolución Cubana*. Vol. 3. Havana: Talleres de Cultural, 1931.

Moreno Fraginals, Manuel. *El ingenio. El complejo económico-social cubano del azúcar*. Vol. 1. Havana: Empresa Consolidada de Artes Gráficas, 1964.

Moscoso, Francisco. *Bibliografía de la conquista y colonización de Puerto Rico: Siglos XV-XVII (1492-1650)*. Río Pedras, Puerto Rico: University of Puerto Rico, 2005.

Moya Pons, Frank. *History of the Caribbean: Plantations, Trade, and War in the Atlantic World*. Princeton, NJ: Markus Wiener Publishers, 2007.

Navarro Azcue, Concepcion. *La abolición de la esclavitud negra en la legislación española, 1870-1886*. Madrid: Instituto de Cooperación Iberoamericana: Ediciones Cultura Hispanica, 1987.

Negrón-Portillo, Mariano, and Raúl Mayo Santana. *La esclavitud urbana en San Juan de Puerto Rico: estudio del Registro de Esclavos de 1872*. Río Pedras, Puerto Rico: Ediciones Huracán: Centro de Investigaciones Sociales, University of Puerto Rico, 1992.

———. *Urban Slavery in San Juan*. Río Pedras, Puerto Rico: Centro de Investigaciones Sociales, University of Puerto Rico, 1999.

Pastrana, F. *Catecismo de geografía de la isla de Puerto Rico*. San

Juan, Puerto Rico: Imprenta Márquez, 1852.

Patterson, Orlando. *The Sociology of Slavery*. London: MacGibbon and Kee, 1967.

Picó, Fernando. *History of Puerto Rico: A Panorama of Its People.* Princeton, NJ: Markus Wiener Publishers, 2006.

Quevedo Báez, Manuel. *Historia de la medicina y ciencia en Puerto Rico*. Vol. 2. Santurce: Asociación Médica de Puerto Rico. Imprenta Soltero, 1946-49.

Rout, Leslie B., Jr. *The African Experience in Spanish America*. Princeton, NJ: Markus Wiener Publishers, 2003.

Ruiz Belvis, S., J. J. Acosta, F. M. Quiñones et al., eds. *Proyecto para la abolición de la esclavitud en Puerto Rico*. San Juan, Puerto Rico: Establecimiento Tipográfico R. Vicente, 1870.

Saco, José Antonio. *La historia de la esclavitud desde los tiempos más remotos hasta nuestros días*. Vol. 4. Paris: Tipografía la Hwe., 1875.

Scarano, Francisco A. *Sugar and Slavery in Puerto Rico: The Plantation Economy of Ponce, 1800-1850*. Madison: University of Wisconsin Press, 1984.

Stedman, J. G. *Narrative of a Five Year Expedition Against Revolted Negroes of Surinam*. Pall Mall J. J. Johnson, St. Paul Church Yard, 1796.

Sued Badillo, Jalil, and Angel López Cantos. *Puerto Rico negro*. Río Piedras, Puerto Rico: Editorial Cultural, 1986.

Torrento, Mariano. *Cuestión importante sobre la esclavitud*. Madrid: Imp. de la Vda. de Jordán e Hijos, 1941.

Turnbull, David. *Travels in West Cuba and with Notices of Puerto Rico and the Slave Trade*. London: Longman, Orme, Brown, Green Longman, 1840.

Williams, Eric. *Capitalism and Slavery*. Chapel Hill: University of North Carolina Press, 1964.

_____. *From Columbus to Castro. The History of the Caribbean: 1492-1967*. London: Andre Deutsch, 1964.

Zips, Werner. *Black Rebels: African-Caribbean Freedom Fighters in Jamaica*. Princeton, NJ: Markus Wiener Publishers, 1999.

Journals

Alvarez Nazario, Manuel. "Procedencias africanas de los *bozales* traídos a Puerto Rico por la trata negra." *La Torre* 8, no. 31 (July-September 1960), p. 107.

Baur, John E. "International Repercussions of the Haitian Revolution." *The Americas* 26 (April 1970), p. 4.

Colón, Edmundo. "Breve reseña del desenvolvimiento de la agricultura en Puerto Rico antes del 1898." *Revista de Agricultura* 8, no. 2 (1922), pp. 49-53.

Oscariz, J. J. "La Rebelión de Bocanigua." *Anuario de Estudios Americanos* (Seville) 28 (1970), pp. 551-81.

Reckford, Mary. "The Jamaican Slave Rebellion of 1831." *Past and Present: A Journal of Historical Studies*, no. 4 (July 1968), p. 191.

Sánchez, Juan. "Cimarrones y palenques en la lucha secular por la libertad." *Bohemia*, no. 41 (October 11, 1974), pp. 4-9.

Newspapers

El Investigador, no. 2, vol. 16, 1815.

Gaceta Oficial de Puerto Rico, 1820-1848.

About the Author

GUILLERMO A. BARALT, Professor of History at the Río Piedras campus of the University of Puerto Rico, holds a doctorate in Latin American History from the University of Chicago. His thesis on slave uprisings in Puerto Rico, *Esclavos rebeldes,* was published by Ediciones Huracán in 1982. It won the 1983 Puerto Rico PEN Club Award and was named the best history text of that year. Other publications include *Azúcar y esclavitud en Toa Baja* (1983); *Yauco o las minas cafetaleras* (1984); and *La Buena Vista: estancia de frutos menores, fabrica de harinas y hacienda cafetalera* (1988). The Association of Caribbean Historians awarded this last work the Elsa Goveia Prize in 1992 for best work of history about the Caribbean, and it appeared in English under the title *Buena Vista: Life and Work on a Puerto Rican Hacienda, 1833-1904. Buena Vista* was chosen to receive a special prize for excellence by the Puerto Rico PEN Club in 1991. *Tradición de Futuro: un siglo de historia del Banco Popular de Puerto Rico* was published in Spanish in 1993, and then in English as *Tradition into the Future.* Three years later, Baralt published *Desde el mirador de Próspero: La vida de Luis A. Ferré, 1904-1968,* and *La razón del equilibrio, 1968-1998.*

Baralt's most recent books include *Al servicio de mi Tierra: Historia de El Nuevo Día* (2002); *The History of the Federal Court in Puerto Rico: 1899-1999* (2004); and *Recuerdos del Porvenir: Historia del Sistema Universitario Ana G. Méndez* (2004).

CHRISTINE AYORINDE, the translator, has spent many years visiting Cuba, researching and writing on Afro-Cuban themes, religion, and questions of national identity. She is the translator of *Afro-Cuban Religions,* by Miguel Barnet; *Cuban Legends,* edited by Salvador Bueno; and *Dominican Cultures: The Making of a Caribbean Society* (2007), edited by Bernardo Vega. Her publications include *Afro-Cuban Religiosity* and *Revolution and National Identity* (2004), as well as chapters in *Identity in the Shadow of Slavery* (2000); *The Yoruba Diaspora in the Atlantic World* (2005); and *Contesting Freedom: Control and Resistance in the Century after Emancipation in the Caribbean* (2005).

CPSIA information can be obtained
at www.ICGtesting.com
Printed in the USA
BVHW081152150620
581543BV00002B/403

9 781558 764637